THE PARAGON ISSUES IN PHILOSOPHY SERIES

At colleges and universities, interest in the traditional areas of philosophy remains strong. Many new currents flow within them, too, but some of these—the rise of cognitive science, for example, or feminist philosophy—went largely unnoticed in undergraduate philosophy courses until the end of the 1980s. The Paragon Issues in Philosophy Series responds to both perennial and newly influential concerns by bringing together a team of able philosophers to address the fundamental issues in philosophy today and to outline the state of contemporary discussion about them.

More than twenty volumes are scheduled; they are organized into three major categories. The first covers the standard topics—metaphysics, theory of knowledge, ethics, and political philosophy—stressing innovative developments in those disciplines. The second focuses on more specialized but still vital concerns in the philosophies of science, religion, history, sport, and other areas. The third category explores new work that relates philosophy and fields such as feminist criticism, medicine, economics, technology, and literature.

The level of writing is aimed at undergraduate students who have little previous experience studying philosophy. The books provide brief but accurate introductions that appraise the state of the art in their fields and show how the history of thought about their topics developed. Each volume is complete in itself but also complements others in the series.

Traumatic change characterizes these last years of the twentieth century: all of it involves philosophical issues. The editorial staff at Paragon House has worked with us to develop this series. We hope it will encourage the understanding needed in our times, which are as complicated and problematic as they are promising.

John K. Roth
Claremont McKenna College

Frederick Sontag
Pomona College

ALSO BY NANCY TUANA

FEMINISM & SCIENCE

THE MISBEGOTTEN MAN: Scientific, Religious, and Philosophical Conceptions of Woman's Nature

WOMAN
AND THE
HISTORY OF
PHILOSOPHY

NANCY TUANA

THE UNIVERSITY OF TEXAS
AT DALLAS

WOMAN AND THE
HISTORY
OF
PHILOSOPHY

PARAGON
ISSUES IN
PHILOSOPHY

FIRST EDITION, 1992

PUBLISHED IN THE UNITED STATES BY
PARAGON HOUSE
90 FIFTH AVENUE
NEW YORK, N.Y. 10011

COPYRIGHT © 1992 BY PARAGON HOUSE

FRONTISPIECE: *SUSANNA AND THE ELDERS* BY ARTEMISIA GENTILESCHI,
1610, POMMERSFELDEN, SCHLOSS WEISSENSTEIN. COURTESY OF FOTO
MARBURG/ART RESOURCE, N.Y.

LIBRARY OF CONGRESS CATALOGING-IN-PUBLICATION DATA
TUANA, NANCY.
    WOMAN AND THE HISTORY OF PHILOSOPHY / NANCY TUANA. — 1ST ED.
        P.   CM. — (PARAGON ISSUES IN PHILOSOPHY)
    INCLUDES BIBLIOGRAPHICAL REFERENCES AND INDEX.
    ISBN 1-55778-194-X
    1. FEMINIST THEORY. 2. PHILOSOPHY. 3. WOMAN (PHILOSOPHY)
    I. TITLE.   II. SERIES.
    HQ1190.T83   1992
    305.42'01—DC20   91-17917
                                                              CIP

MANUFACTURED IN THE UNITED STATES OF AMERICA

FOR J. F. CARLETON—
FRIEND, LOVER, PARTNER.

CONTENTS

PREFACE

Having taught and written, not to mention living and breathing, feminist theory for the last fifteen years, I am pleased at the changes I have witnessed in the university curricula. Feminist critiques and theories, which were originally looked at with suspicion and marginalized in the humanities, are now receiving attention, if not respect. The fact that the editors of this series, John Roth and Frederick Sontag, had the insight to acknowledge the importance of feminist philosophy and include it in the Paragon Issues in Philosophy Series is a sign of this recognition.

But I fear that at the same time that feminist theory is being welcomed into the academy, it is being marginalized in another way. My anxiety arises out of an experience that I find all too common. I am frequently contacted by colleagues in philosophy who are interested in including feminist perspectives in their classes but who have little background in the area. After describing the topic of their course, they ask if there is a book or collection of articles that might be appropriate to include within their class that would represent the feminist viewpoint. Explaining that there is no one feminist viewpoint, but rather a variety of feminist theories, I offer a list of readings that represent the spectrum of current feminist scholarship. The response to my suggestions is surprisingly uniform. In designing the class, the instructor will select one week, usually toward the end of the term, labeling it "Feminism and Epistemology" or "Feminism and Moral Theory" or "Feminism and the Philosophy of Science," as is appropriate for the specific class, and assign a book or series of articles to be read for that week.

Despite the good intentions of my colleagues, such a practice perpetuates the marginalization of feminist theory. First, it seldom gives recognition to the fact that feminist theory does not consist of a singular theoretical framework, but includes a variety of different and often competing methodologies. Many feminists have attempted to dispel this misunderstanding by offering clear overviews of the multifaceted nature of feminist theory. See, for example, Rosemarie Tong's excellent *Feminist Thought: A Comprehensive Introduction* (Boulder: Westview, 1989). Second, such a practice of "including" feminist theory in the traditional philosophy course also marginalizes it by treating feminist critiques as simply raising additional issues for consideration (issues that apparently can be sufficiently considered in a week's time). It is this latter practice that most concerns me. One point that many feminists quite clearly and resolutely advance is that feminist critiques of philosophy require more than simple modifications of philosophical methods and questions. They necessitate extensive transformations of the discipline itself. It is this point that is too often overlooked when a text on feminist thought is "added into" the traditional curriculum.

One of my goals in writing this book has been to curtail the second component of marginalization. My analyses of canonical philosophers are designed to demonstrate that feminist critiques of traditional philosophy will require such transformations. I will argue that we cannot simply "patch up" Descartes' theory of rationality or Kant's theory of morality to correct the gender biases uncovered by feminist critiques of these theories. One of my central concerns will be to expose the ways in which such gender biases are woven into the very categories of philosophy. My point is not that we have to give up doing philosophy, but that if we are to remove the sexism inherent in the categories of philosophy, the philosophy we do will have to be significantly different.

I have written this book in order to empower readers. I begin by outlining a reading strategy designed to reveal the pattern of gender assumptions embedded within the central concepts of philosophy; then I illustrate this strategy by applying it to selected philosophers and topics in my subsequent chapters. My intent is to offer the reader a different way of attending to the texts of philosophy than is taught in the typical classroom. My desire is not simply to provide a set of "facts" about the beliefs and theories of certain philosophers, but to demonstrate the power and importance of this alternative way of reading philosophy.

Although my analyses of the various philosophers and topics are careful and detailed, it is impossible for my examination to be exhaustive. If I am successful, my arguments will stimulate readers' desire to know more about the impact of gender assumptions upon the practice of philosophy. To respond to this, I have provided suggestions for further reading at the end of each chapter. These lists are selective and designed to provide readers unfamiliar with feminist scholarship additional resources for investigation of the philosophers or topics covered in the chapter.* A more extensive bibliography is

---

* The selections from primary texts listed at the end of chapters are not exhaustive of the comments of the specific philosophers on the subject of woman or the feminine, but they do constitute, in my opinion, the central core of texts relevant to these issues in the work of each.

included at the end of the book. A companion anthology, *Feminism and Philosophy: The Essential Readings*, edited by Nancy Tuana and Rosemarie Tong, soon to be available from Paragon House, contains selections that reflect the diversity of feminist critiques, and their impact upon traditional philosophy.

The ideas and arguments I present in this book are the result of many years of reading feminist scholarship, attending meetings of the Society for Women in Philosophy, and hours of conversations with friends. I have made every effort to cite those articles and books that have been most influential on my thinking. To those friends and colleagues who lovingly attended to my thoughts and ideas in this book, I offer my warmest thanks; my ideas and arguments are far tighter thanks to their comments, and my spirit is stronger due to their care. Carol Adams not only read and commented on every chapter, she offered me much appreciated companionship and wonderful vegan dinners throughout the long and often difficult process of writing this book. Laurie Shrage and Elizabeth Spelman reviewed each chapter with thoughtful concern. Their comments and questions were both insightful and stimulating. Victor Worsfold assisted me with a number of thorny problems I encountered in thinking through the moral theories of Kant and Hume. I received many helpful suggestions and equally helpful emotional support from William Cowling, Paula England, Robin Jarrett, Zsuzsanna Ozsvath, Judith Piper, Karen Prager, Holly Silk, Deborah Stott, and Marilyn Waligore. I was also blessed with a patient and caring editor, Jo Glorie. Her support and encouragement of my work, as well as her loving attention to my needs during a time of birth as well as a time of war, kept up my spirits on many a difficult day.

CHAPTER ONE

READING PHILOSOPHY AS A WOMAN

SUSANNA AND THE ELDERS

Susanna was the wife of Joakim of Babylon. She was renowned for her great beauty. This beautiful wife had righteous parents who taught her to fear the Lord.

As Joakim was both very rich and the most honored of all men in Babylon, his house was a meeting place. Among his many guests were two Elders that the people had appointed as judges to govern them. Because of their frequent visits, the Elders often saw Susanna walking in the garden of her husband; they began to desire her.

Confessing their lust to one another, the Elders conspired to entrap her by hiding in the garden and waiting until Susanna was alone. Emerging from the house wishing to bathe, Susanna sent her maids indoors to fetch ointments. The moment she was alone, the two Elders sprang out of their hiding place and demanded that she lie with them. They threatened that if she refused, they would denounce her publicly, claiming to have caught her in the arms of a young man, a charge punishable by death. "Susanna sighed deeply, and said, 'I am hemmed in on every side. For if I do this thing, it is death for me: and if I do not, I shall not escape your hands. I choose not to do it and to fall into your hands, rather than to sin in the sight of the Lord.' "[1] And Susanna cried out loudly, preventing the rape.

The Elders testified against Susanna. The assembly believed them because they were Elders of the people and judges. Susanna was condemned to death. Susanna cried out, "These men have borne false witness against me. And now I am to die! Yet I have done none of the things that they have wickedly invented against me!"[2]

She was saved at the last minute by Daniel, who demanded a new trial. By separating the Elders and interrogating them individually, he received conflicting stories, thereby proving that the Elders bore false witness against Susanna. The Elders were put to death for their wickedness. All the people rejoiced. We are told that Joakim and all of Susanna's kindred praised God *for their daughter "because nothing shameful was found in her."*[3] *We are told that from that day onward Daniel had a great reputation among the people.**

❧

A woman reading philosophy† must decide where to place herself. When the philosopher speaks of the nature of man, informs us of the rationality of man, provides us with the rules a man must follow in order to act morally, does the woman include herself within the referent of the term "man"? Often, without thinking about it, we assume that "man" is used with its gender-neutral meaning and read ourself into the text. But the doubt persists. The word carries both meanings regardless of the philosopher's intention and thus carries our exclusion alongside our inclusion.

Because of the ambiguity of the term "man," the texts of philosophy are experienced differently by women than they are by men. Take the following passage from Hegel:

A man actualizes himself only in becoming something definite, i.e. something specifically particularized; this means . . . to make oneself a member of one of the moments of civil society by one's own act, through one's energy, industry, and skill, to maintain oneself in this position, and to fend for oneself only through this process of mediating oneself with the universal, while in this way gaining recognition both in one's own eyes and in the eyes of others.‡

For a man reading this text, this statement asserts the equation of maleness with humanity. Whether or not he agrees with Hegel's view, in reading this passage he experiences his own identity with the universal, that is, with the paradigmatic human, simply because he is male. The woman reading this text is left with the question of her inclusion. Is she included because she is human? Or excluded because she is female?

* The frontispiece and the cover are both depictions of the story of Susanna and the Elders.

† When speaking of philosophy in this chapter, I am referring to canonical Western philosophy. Although the academy is beginning to expand its offerings beyond the list of "great philosophers" taught in the typical history of philosophy course, the majority of classes and readings remain focused on this canon.

‡ *Hegel's Philosophy of Right*, trans. T. M. Knox (London: Oxford University Press, 1967), p. 207. My particular expression of the problem of reading Hegel's text is in part due to Knox's translation. This passage opens with *"Der Mensch"* ("A human"), not *"Ein Mann"* ("A man"). It is Knox who renders it into English as "A man. . . ." Still, as I will argue in detail in Chapter Five, Hegel excludes woman from such actualization. So even though Hegel used the supposedly gender-neutral *"Der Mensch,"* his usage of the term was nevertheless gender-marked.

But I have stated the problem too simply. Although, as I will illustrate in Chapter Five, when Hegel here refers to "a man" he does in fact exclude women, his referent also excludes non-European men. Race, as well as class, is often a factor in exclusion. Although I will focus in this book upon the ways in which a woman's gender affects the issue of her exclusion from the texts of philosophy, it is also imperative to be aware of issues of race and class. Issues of exclusion are often structured differently for race and class than for gender. Hegel's exclusion of non-European men from the above passage has a form different than that of his exclusion of non-European and European women. He saw the exclusion of non-European men as a contingent fact of history. That is, according to Hegel, non-European men had not yet evolved to the point where they were capable of actualizing themselves. But he did not deny their inherent capacity for such actualization. The difference of gender is significant, for in Hegel's account, all women, regardless of race or class, would never be capable of such actualization. Thus women's exclusion is absolute. Nevertheless, issues of gender, race, and class are interrelated in that philosophical and scientific justifications for the superiority of one group over another, justifications which have varied significantly over the centuries, have been influenced by and have in turn reinforced racist and classist biases, as well as sexist biases.[4] Hence, my analysis of gender exclusion would be enriched by studying it alongside concomitant examinations of exclusions based on race or class within the history of philosophy.[5]

The problems of the woman reading philosophy intensify when the talk turns to woman. She has no doubt that she is the subject of the discourse, but she cannot recognize herself in what she reads. The woman reading Aristotle cannot identify with Aristotle's description of woman, for his construction of woman's nature entails that she is unable to undertake the very thing in which she is engaged—philosophy. The woman reading Hegel in order to identify the nature of the good state cannot locate herself in the text as woman, for he tells her that woman is unable to achieve awareness of the universality of the state. The woman searching for a moral philosophy in reading Kant cannot internalize what he says about woman, for to do so would mean that she would have to accept that she is precluded from moral agency and should therefore cease her investigation.*

The woman reading philosophy soon finds that she is presented as "Other" rather than as "Subject" in the texts of the philosophers. Consider the following passage from Rousseau:

Woman, who is weak and who sees nothing outside the house, estimates and judges the forces she can put to work to make up for her weakness, and those forces are

---

* My supports for these claims are to be found in Chapters Two, Five, and Four respectively.

men's passions. Her science of mechanics is more powerful than ours: all her levers unsettle the human heart. She must have the art to make us want to do everything which her sex cannot do by itself and which is necessary or agreeable to it.[6]

It is to a man, albeit a man of the white European upper class, that Rousseau addresses this passage. For the man who reads this text, whether or not he agrees with Rousseau, whether or not the above passage represents his experience, the discourse constructs him as Subject. It is he to whom Rousseau speaks. The woman reading the text realizes immediately that she is the Object of the discourse; she is presented as Other. She is being talked about, but is not addressed. The woman reading Rousseau finds herself confronted by a paradox. She is, on the one hand, being defined as Other; on the other hand, she is invited to identify herself as male, yet all the while being told that to be male is to be not female.

The woman reading philosophy thus finds herself alienated from the text. To insert herself into the text—to insist that she is capable of rational thought, to perceive herself as a moral agent, to believe that she too can understand and participate in the workings of the state—is to believe that she can act "like a man," for, as I will demonstrate in the following chapters, each of these abilities is defined within philosophy as "male." At times, the option of acting "like a man" may seem acceptable to the woman reading philosophy. We attempt to suppress our knowledge that we are being defined as Other, and we say to ourselves, "Women, after all, are capable of anything men are." But this "solution" often only adds to our alienation. As we attempt to force ourselves into the categories so defined, many of us discover that these categories omit qualities and abilities we value, qualities and abilities defined as "feminine"—emotion, empathy, connectedness—qualities and abilities which are a part of our conception of ourselves as women and as human which we do not believe should be rejected. In other words, we discover that philosophy omits the experiences of being women.

For the woman reading philosophy, this alienation can be more or less apparent. It often manifests itself in an amorphous discomfort we experience while reading the text, something difficult to express, an open-ended disquiet with no obvious source. As a woman reading philosophy, I experienced this unease for years. The writing of this book has been my journey to uncover the source of my discomfort. I believe that in order to reveal the basis of women's alienation from the texts of philosophy, we must read "as a woman."

Reading as a woman involves a particular focus of attention. This focus includes an examination of the ways in which the conception of woman is being constructed by the text. What, for example, are we told, either explicitly or implicitly, about woman's nature? And what of woman's abilities? Are there certain physical or mental pursuits that women are seen as more capable of than others? For what types of roles are women depicted as suited? How do these compare to the roles perceived as suitable for men? Reading as a woman also requires attention to the construction of the feminine. That is, how do traits and characteristics perceived as feminine compare in treatment to those defined as masculine? What role do such traits play within activities and faculties a philosopher sees as central to being human?

Reading in this way, with this focus of attention, reveals the ways in which philosophers' culturally inherited beliefs about women and the feminine affect their theories. We very quickly discover that the discourses of philosophy are not gender-neutral. Questions like those listed above provide a framework for exposing the ways in which gender assumptions are imbedded within philosophical texts.

Many will be tempted to object that a philosopher's gender biases, although perhaps historically interesting, are not philosophically significant. Such individuals might be willing to admit that philosophers would be influenced by the sexist attitudes of their culture and historical period and would, in descriptions of woman's nature and role, reproduce these biases. But these individuals would object that although we might be moved to castigate a philosopher for his lack of enlightenment on this point, we must allow that he was, after all, a man of his times.* What remains implicit in this objection is the belief that a philosopher's gender biases, although perhaps reprehensible, are independent of his larger theoretical framework.

It is this hidden assumption, that a philosopher's gender biases are irrelevant to his philosophical system, that is undermined by the reading strategy that I propose. Focusing attention on the subject of woman exposes the fact that philosophers have inscribed gender biases on the central categories of their theories—what it is to be human, to be rational, to be moral, to be a political agent. Reading as a woman we discover that we cannot treat the philosophical narrative as offering a universal perspective. Philosophers, like other theorists, privilege some experiences and ways of seeing over others.

The ability to read as a woman as I am defining it is a strategy open to women and men alike. It is a form of critical reading with an emphasis on gender issues. To illustrate this reading strategy, let us return to the story of Susanna. The story is typically read as exemplifying the theme of salvation or deliverance: Susanna, falsely accused by evil men, is saved at the last minute by Daniel, the agent of God. The story is interpreted as an assurance that those, like Susanna, who have faith in God will ultimately be protected

* Since my discussion is limited to canonical philosophers, the masculine pronoun is appropriate.

from harm. We perceive the evilness of the Elders in the lust of their gaze and in their acts of deceit, and we admire Daniel for his wisdom and shrewdness. Such a reading focuses on the content of the story. The gender of the reader, we are to suppose, is irrelevant. But is it?

By acknowledging the fact that I am a woman reading the story of Susanna, not a generic, genderless reader, I begin to experience a tension. Where do I place myself in the text? With whom do I identify? I am initially tempted to identify with Susanna—a woman so courageous she would face death and dishonor rather than submit to rape. But then I become aware of how Susanna is being defined within the text. Her act of resistance, an act I see as one of bravery, is minimized. When the false witness of the Elders is revealed, no one expresses compassion for Susanna, and no one sings her praise. It is God who is praised, Daniel who is honored. But is it not Susanna who is the hero of this text? Why then is her courage suppressed? In attempting to place myself within the text, I experience a tension between my image of Susanna and that conveyed by the text.

To identify the source of this tension, I will attend to the story of Susanna in a different way. I focus on what I am being told about woman's nature, about woman's proper role. To see this, I must become aware not only of the gaze of the Elders who construct Susanna as an object of their sexual desire but also of the gaze from outside the garden walls, the gaze that defines Susanna as woman. And I must resist this gaze.

In the Gospel of Daniel, Susanna is depicted as a virtuous woman, a woman to be emulated (by other women). But look at how this woman, Susanna, is constructed within this text. Susanna is defined as a wife. She has no role, no function but as wife. She owns nothing. We are told that the garden is Joakim's, and we must presume that so too is the house, and perhaps the children, and perhaps, too, Susanna. Her beauty is emphasized. Does that make her a better wife? More virtuous? Or just more likely to be desired by men? In reading the text, it becomes clear that a good wife is to have nothing shameful in her. But when it is found that Susanna had nothing shameful in her, no one praised or applauded her. Rather they praised God, thereby crediting another agent for her honorable behavior. Are women incapable of independent agency? Or perhaps it is just expected that the good wife will have nothing shameful in her. Maybe this is one of those traits only commented on when missing. And we are told that Susanna fears the Lord. It is this fear that enables her to resist the Elders. But she is not praised for it by the people. Only the men, or rather the good men, are praised or honored. Are women, even good women, perhaps not deserving of praise or of honor?

By reading in this way, the source of my discomfort becomes clear. I resist the definition of woman solely as wife. I am angered by the exclusion of woman from praise or honor. Imbedded within the text is a particular image of woman, an image which is often overlooked yet is unconsciously accepted while we focus on other aspects of the narrative. The story of Susanna is traditionally read as illustrating the power of faith. Accepting this interpretation and similarly disregarding the way in which woman is constructed within this text serves to perpetuate this conception of woman. My discomfort arises from my refusal to ignore the ways in which woman is defined within this text.

In reading as a woman it is important to shift our focus in this way, that is, to privilege the conception of woman being offered, often implicitly, within the text. In this way beliefs about the nature of woman can be identified and made subject to critical analysis. In addition, such a shift makes the relations, if any, between the concepts of femininity and masculinity an object of critical attention. And equally important, such a reading enables us to determine if certain traits or abilities are being defined as gendered, that is, marked as feminine or masculine. Such a process often carries a text beyond its stated topic by examining the assumptions behind it. Reading as a woman we become aware of the fact that the texts of philosophy are neither autonomous or universal. A philosopher writes from a particular perspective and is influenced by the cultural values she or he has inherited. Thus to understand a philosophical text, we must read it within the framework of this larger context. In this book, I will focus on one aspect of this context, the question of gender.

My conception of reading as a woman, then, is about the reader's focus of attention. It has nothing to do with one's genes or the parts of one's body. It has rather to do with a concern for enabling the varieties of women's experiences to be included within the paradigms of human experience. But this can only be done if the reader takes control of the reading experience and reads the text differently than the author intended it to be read, that is, reads it as a woman without putting oneself in the position of the Other. To do this, the text must be read in such a way as to undermine the presuppositions which define woman as not male, as limited, and as Other.

My goal in writing this book is to enable one to read as a woman. To do this, I privilege "woman"; that is, I take a philosopher's views on the nature of woman as an important basis for understanding her or his philosophical system. My aim is to reveal the process of definition of woman in Western culture as not male, as Other. I will also endeavor to explain how the discourse of exclusion works even when a philosopher does not mention the topic of woman.

It is my thesis that a systematic examination of the subject of woman in the history of philosophy reveals a set of assumptions having to do not only with the nature of woman but also with the concept of the "feminine."* In using the terms "feminine," "female," "masculine," and "male," I am referring to traits, characteristics, and activities historically associated with women or with men. But this history of associations is neither static nor consistent.[7] Recognizing this fact, I attempt to be sensitive to the meanings and relations of these terms contained within the writings of each thinker. Whenever possible I examine a philosopher's explicit delineations of woman's nature or of femininity. But this is only a beginning. To understand a theorist's conception of femininity or masculinity, one must read between the lines, with careful attention to unspoken assumptions.

One of the most basic gender assumptions found throughout the philosophical canon is the tenet that man is the true form of humanity; that is, masculinity is equated with humanness.† This axiom is then implicitly inscribed on all of the categories central to philosophy. The definitions of rationality and of morality, for example, often emphasize traits which are viewed as masculine and minimize or exclude traits seen as feminine.‡ The practice of excluding the feminine in turn reinforces the view of woman as Other and as inferior by devaluing her capacities and her achievements, and thereby justifies her exclusion from what are considered the higher realms of human endeavor.

In constructing this text, I have elected to focus only on canonical philosophers, that is, those philosophers who have come to be seen as presenting well-developed and highly influential philosophies. I do not intend to imply that these philosophers are the best or that they together represent the entire range of possible philosophical systems. I focus on them because these are the philosophers who have been repeatedly anthologized and who are regularly studied in the Western academy.[8] It is my conviction that understanding the gender system in their writings reveals a pattern of depreciation of woman and the feminine that is still prevalent in much of contemporary Western philosophy.

I have not attempted to survey the entirety of the history of philosophy,

---

* It is my position that femininity and masculinity are socially constructed. In other words, I do not accept the essentialist view that a woman's femininity is an innate characteristic. Nevertheless, I caution against the view that biology is irrelevant. Although for the purposes of this analysis, I remain neutral regarding the very problematic question of the source or causes of the association of women and femininity, I caution the reader against falling into the quagmire of nature/nurture debates. It is my opinion that it is the dichotomy between biology and culture or environment that is at fault. See my "Re-Fusing Nature/Nurture," in *Hypatia Reborn*, ed. Azizah al-Hibri and Margaret Simons (Bloomington: Indiana University Press, 1990).

† As I will later illustrate, this bias goes hand in hand with the belief that some groups of people are superior to others. Because of this not all men in fact achieve full humanity, but *only* men, and no women, are capable of it.

‡ These claims receive support in Chapters Three and Four.

for that would condemn the analysis of each philosopher to a thumbnail sketch and would require simplification to the point of distortion. I chose instead to organize the text thematically and develop my analysis by selecting pairs of philosophers that represent different positions in the spectrum of thought concerning each topic.

I begin in Chapter Two by examining the equation of humanness with maleness, that is, the belief that man is the true form of humanity and that woman is inferior to him, lacking in just those traits which are seen as most distinctively human. To construct this chapter, I contrast the philosophies of Plato and Aristotle on the subject of woman. A comparison of their positions is revealing, their similarities being as important as their differences. Moreover, despite Plato's reputation as the "first feminist,"[9] he, like Aristotle, views woman as inferior to man. But there is an important difference in their convictions concerning the origin of woman's inferiority to man. Aristotle, like the majority of philosophers after him, associates woman's defects with her reproductive role. Plato, in contrast to Aristotle, denies that woman's generative role has any effect on her abilities. However, I will demonstrate that although Plato denies the importance of the bodily differences between the sexes, he posits significant differences between the souls of women and men. Despite their differences concerning the cause of woman's inferiority, Plato and Aristotle agree on its effects. In particular, both argue that woman is less capable than man of developing the "higher" faculties of rationality and morality.

In the subsequent two chapters, I examine the philosophical construction of woman in terms of theories of rationality and morality. In Chapter Three I address the issue of woman's rational abilities and examine the extent to which philosophical theories of rationality privilege characteristics perceived as masculine. To frame this chapter, I compare the philosophies of Descartes and Rousseau. Although their conceptions of rationality are similar in that both of these theorists associate traits viewed as masculine with reason, they differ in their response to the emotions and the passions, traits they associate with the feminine. Descartes' theory denigrates emotions, condemning them to the realm of the irrational. Rousseau, on the other hand, argues for an integration of reason and emotion, seeing emotion as reason's guide. My focus in this chapter is on the gender implications of these two models of rationality. That is, I analyze how woman fares when the emotions are seen as antithetical to reason versus when the emotions are viewed as reason's guide.

In Chapter Four I turn to theories of morality, the second of the two "higher" faculties. For my comparison I have selected the moral philosophies of Kant and Hume. Kant, accepting the Cartesian opposition of reason and emotion, argues that an action is moral only if it is based solely on reason.

Hume, unlike Kant, does not exclude the emotions from the moral realm, but rather founds moral action on the sentiments and affections of humans. My concerns and my questions in this chapter are similar to those of the previous chapter. Is morality being conceived as male? Are women viewed as incapable or less capable than men of moral agency? The comparison of these two competing moral theories offers a clear illustration of the variety of ways in which woman can be excluded from philosophy.

Beliefs concerning woman's capacity for rational thought or moral agency directly affect the construction of political theory and philosophies concerning woman's proper role. If participation in the public realm of government is seen as requiring possession of well-developed rational and moral capacities, then theories of woman's nature which define woman as less capable than man in just these areas will have a direct effect on a philosopher's view of woman's proper role in the state. In Chapter Five I compare the political philosophy of Locke with that of Hegel. I selected Locke as a representative of the liberalist view that all individuals, women and men alike, in the original state of nature are free and equal, and that relations of authority are the result of rational consent. I contrast his political philosophy with that of Hegel, who subscribes to the tenet that the natures of woman and man are different and complementary. My concern is to see how this difference in their basic tenets affects their views of woman's proper role in the state. In addition I am concerned to examine the value each theorist places on what he perceives as woman's proper role. In this chapter I argue that the prejudice that man is the true form of humanity is so strong that both philosophers contravened their most basic doctrines in order to uphold it.

I conclude this examination with a brief discussion of the feminist challenge to philosophy. I discuss some of the contemporary feminist responses to the denigration of woman's abilities and activities in the texts of philosophy, as well as to the tendency in philosophy to associate rationality and morality with traits viewed as masculine. Although my discussion is selective, my intent is to end the book with an outline of the consequences of reading as a woman, that is, the realization that some of the central categories of philosophy must be transformed in order to include woman and the variety of women's experiences.[10]

My book is not exhaustive. I could not discuss all canonical philosophers; thus there are numerous positions omitted from this investigation. Nor could I examine all themes of importance to the conceptualization of woman in philosophy. What I have provided is a blueprint for such investigations. My goal in writing this book has been to offer my reader the tools for conducting this type of reading every time she or he picks up a philosophical text. By focusing my analysis on the fundamental assumptions concerning woman's nature which are uniformly accepted by diverse theorists, I hope I have provided measures for reading philosophy as a woman. Similarly by focusing on the types of strategies that lead to the exclusion of woman from the texts of these philosophers, I have intended to sensitize readers to similar exclusions in other writings. Thus, I have written this book not only to reveal the gender system in the philosophy of selected theorists but also to introduce readers to a different strategy for reading philosophy that extends far beyond the limits of this particular text.

In this opening chapter I stress the latter aspect of my book because I see it as crucial to the transformation of philosophy. I believe that my analyses of Plato, Aristotle, Descartes, Rousseau, Hume, Kant, Locke, and Hegel reveal the complexity of woman's exclusion from their philosophies. Reading my chapters will enhance one's understanding of these theorists' philosophical systems, for, as I will demonstrate, their position on the nature of man cannot be fully understood without also comprehending their conception of woman and the feminine. Nevertheless, if the reader does not also walk away from this book with an awareness of the importance of reading philosophy differently than she or he has been taught in the academy, then I have not been fully successful. This book is not simply about the history of philosophy. The assumptions about woman's nature that I discuss in these chapters, as well as the ways in which woman is excluded from the central categories of philosophy, still function within modern philosophical systems and debates. We can question or reject such prejudices only if we first unveil them and understand their effects on our own beliefs. Thus, if you use this book well, it will serve as the basis for a transformation of how you read and do philosophy.

Remember the gaze outside the garden wall. It was not only the Elders who condemned Susanna.

FURTHER READING

READING AS A WOMAN

Cantrell, Carol H. "Analogy as Destiny: Cartesian Man and the Woman Reader." *Hypatia: A Journal of Feminist Philosophy* 5, 2 (1990): 7–19.

Doeuff, Michele le. "Ants and Women, or Philosophy without Borders." *Philosophy* 21, supplement (1987): 41–54.

Flynn, Elizabeth A., and Patrocinio P. Schweickart, eds. *Gender and Reading: Essays on Readers, Texts, and Contexts.* Baltimore: Johns Hopkins University Press, 1986.

Fuss, Diana. *Essentially Speaking: Feminism, Nature & Difference.* New York: Routledge, 1989. Chapter 2, "Reading like a Feminist."

Meese, Elizabeth. *(Ex)Tensions: Re-Figuring Feminist Criticism.* Urbana: University of Illinois Press, 1990.

Newton, Judith, and Deborah Rosenfelt. *Feminist Criticism and Social*

Change: Sex, Class and Race in Literature and Culture. New York: Methuen, 1985.

Wall, Cheryl A. *Changing Our Own Words: Essays on Criticism, Theory and Writing by Black Women*. New Brunswick: Rutgers University Press, 1989.

FEMINISM AND PHILOSOPHY

Code, Lorraine, Sheila Mullett, and Christine Overall, eds. *Feminist Perspectives: Philosophical Essays on Method and Morals*. Toronto: University of Toronto Press, 1988.

Garry, Ann, and Marilyn Pearsall, eds. *Women, Knowledge and Reality: Explorations in Feminist Philosophy*. Boston: Unwin Hyman, 1989.

Griffiths, Morwenna, and Margaret Whitford, eds. *Feminist Perspectives in Philosophy*. Bloomington: Indiana University Press, 1988.

Grimshaw, Jean. *Philosophy and Feminist Thinking*. Minneapolis: University of Minnesota Press, 1986.

Harding, Sandra, and Merrill B. Hintikka, eds. *Discovering Reality: Feminist Perspectives on Epistemology, Metaphysics, Methodology and Philosophy of Science*. Dordrecht: D. Reidel, 1983.

Jaggar, Alison M. *Feminist Politics and Human Nature*. Totowa, NJ: Rowman & Allanheld, 1983.

———. "How Can Philosophy Be Feminist?" *APA Newsletter on Feminism and Philosophy*, April 1988, pp. 4–8.

Nye, Andrea. *Feminist Theory and the Philosophies of Man*. London: Croom Helm, 1988.

Pearsall, Marilyn, ed. *Women and Values: Readings in Recent Feminist Philosophy*. Belmont, CA: Wadsworth, 1986.

Tong, Rosemarie. *Feminist Thought: A Comprehensive Introduction*. Boulder: Westview Press, 1989.

See also bibliographies contained in issues of the American Philosophical Association *Newsletter on Feminism and Philosophy*.

CHAPTER TWO

THE SECOND SEX

A prevalent theme in Western philosophical thought is the view of woman as inferior to man—as the weaker, secondary sex. As I will document in later chapters, woman is seen as lacking in just those areas judged as distinctively human: the rational and moral faculties. Although this image of woman has roots well back to antiquity, the tenet of the inferiority of woman receives a systematic examination in the works of the two classical philosophers whose writings most influenced Western thought, Plato (427–347 B.C.E.) and Aristotle (384–322 B.C.E.).

A comparison of the views of Plato and Aristotle concerning the nature of woman is revealing in that it discloses two quite different methods for defending the premise of woman's inferiority. Aristotle's philosophy is an illustration of the approach most prevalent in the history of philosophy. It is his position that biological differences are the fundamental cause of variations in the natures and abilities of women and men. Aristotle focuses upon woman's reproductive role in his demonstration of her biological inferiority to man and, in turn, implicates this role as the cause of a series of weaknesses and incapacities in woman's nature and character. In the centuries following Aristotle, his views concerning woman's inferiority would be frequently repeated in the writings of scientists and religious thinkers, as well as those of other philosophers.[1]

Although Plato's conclusions concerning woman's inferiority are quite similar to those of Aristotle, his explanation of the cause of this inferiority is markedly different. While Aristotle devotes his attention to a study of the physiology of women and men, Plato largely ignores the question of the physical differences between them, arguing that the question of an individual's abilities or character is to be answered by inquiring into the nature of her or his soul rather than looking at the configuration of her or his body. Having dismissed bodily differences, Plato focuses his analysis on the nature of the souls of women and men.

Despite this dissimilarity, Plato and Aristotle agree on one fundamental principle: the male is the true form of humanity. Although I will touch upon what they perceive to be the implications of this "fact" for woman's role, my emphasis in this chapter will be to reveal and carefully examine the system of beliefs associated with their equation of maleness with humanness. In subsequent chapters, I will trace the manner in which this tenet became the foundation for theories concerning woman's inferior rational and moral capacities, which were in turn used as the basis for justifying the exclusion of women from full participation in the public realm of the state.

FALLEN SOULS: PLATO

Plato's *Timaeus* contains a creation myth in which the creation of woman is depicted as both temporally and metaphysically secondary. In this dialogue, Plato recounts the creation of the universe and of the beings that populate it. The divine being formed the universe from a mixture of the four elements: earth, air, fire, and water. To create man, the divine being added the soul of the universe to a mixture of these four elements and then "divided the whole mixture into souls equal in number to the stars and assigned each soul to a star." (*Timaeus* 41d.) Each soul was implanted in a body and given the faculty of sensation and the emotions, including those of love, fear, and anger. In the first birth, each man would be equal in perfection to all others, for god would allow "no one [to] suffer a disadvantage at his hands." (*Timaeus* 41e.) In this way, the race of men came into being.

Plato thus envisioned a world without women, for in their primordial state, all humans were male. Women come into existence only in the later births. Although created equally perfect, each man had to choose how to live his life and how to use his faculties. Plato explained that a man's fate was determined by how he dealt with his passions and how he responded to his bodily impressions. "If they conquered these they would live righteously, and if they were conquered by them, unrighteously." (*Timaeus* 42b.) The soul of the man who conquered his emotions and used his intellect to govern his sensations would, upon the death of his body, return to his appointed star, whereupon he would have a "blessed" existence. But the man who failed in this would be reborn as a woman. "At the second birth he would pass into a woman, and if, when in that state of being, he did not desist from evil, he would continually be changed into some brute who resembled him the evil nature which he had acquired." (*Timaeus* 42b–c.)

On this account, woman's existence is not only temporally secondary, it is metaphysically secondary. That is, not only does woman come into existence after man, but she is also less perfect than man. She exists as the result of a lack of control, and is the punishment for being tied to the world of sensations.

Woman is a degeneration of the original state of being. She is a decline, a further estrangement from the happiness of the heavens. Man, thus, is the true form of humankind; woman is an inferior copy. "As human nature was of two kinds, the superior race . . . would hereafter be called man." (*Timaeus* 42a.) The inferior race is woman.*

What is most important to notice about Plato's creation myth is the valuations contained within it, for these will continue to be a central element of conceptions of woman's nature for many centuries. In the *Timaeus*, Plato makes it clear that the passions must be "conquered" by reason or man will lose perfection. Plato envisions the soul as composed of three parts or faculties: the rational, the spiritual, and the appetitive. He depicts these faculties as arranged in a hierarchy of perfection, with that part of the soul that "reckons and reasons," the rational, as being the most perfect, and the appetitive, "that with which it loves, hungers, thirsts, and feels the flutter and titillation of other desires," as the least perfect. (*Republic* 439d.) Plato similarly perceives the soul as more perfect than the body, seeing the body as associated with the appetitive faculty. In fact, he argues that living righteously requires that the rational faculty and the spirit work together to control the appetitive faculty, "lest, by being filled and infected with the so-called pleasures associated with the body and waxing big and strong, it may . . . overturn the entire life of all." (*Republic* 442a–b.) This, however, bodes ill for women. For they, originating from "those who were cowards or led unrighteous lives" in their first birth, will be less capable of such control.

Plato's conception of woman as temporally and metaphysically secondary is not unique. In fact, he would have been well aware of the *Theogony* of Hesiod, in which woman was envisioned in a similar fashion. According to Hesiod, the first generations consisted only of men. Womankind was created later, to be a punishment to mankind because of the deeds of Prometheus, the champion of man, who opposed the counsels of Zeus. "Zeus who roars on high made women to be an evil for mortal men, helpmates in deeds of harshness."[2] Plato refined and developed this conception of woman by placing it within a clearly delineated metaphysical system.

Plato espouses a metaphysic based on hierarchy, in which traits are de-

---

* The *Timaeus* is not unique in possessing this image of women. In the *Laws*, Plato employs similar images. For example, when discussing the just punishment for a soldier who throws down his weapons in order to escape death, Plato argues that the most fair punishment would be for such a man to be changed into a woman. In addition he refers to the man as a coward who possesses an "unmanly" spirit. (*Laws* 944d–945a.) In other words, Plato is arguing that a soldier who is a coward possesses the spirit of a woman, an inferior spirit. As I will illustrate, this claim is complicated by Plato's views concerning superior and inferior classes of people. The final position is not that all women are inferior to all men, but rather that within any specified class, its women are inferior to its men.

fined in terms of their relative degrees of estrangement from the divine and from that out of which order evolves, that is, from *nous*. So, for example, reason is seen as closer to the divine and more perfect than emotion. The soul is viewed as separate from and superior to body. The unchanging realm of the gods is viewed as perfect, the changing realm of the body imperfect. In this way, differences are defined in terms of dichotomy—reason/emotion, soul/body, essence/accident—in which one of the pair is privileged over the other, that is, is seen as more perfect. As I will document in the following chapters, this metaphysic underlies Western philosophy and has important implications for conceptions of woman's nature as well as theories concerning the "proper" relationships between men and women. For Plato, it constitutes the foundation for claiming that women are an "inferior race."

Plato metaphorically extends this gender difference even to the makeup of the soul. Man, Plato explains, was created with two souls, an immortal soul and a mortal soul. The immortal soul "dwells at the top of the body," the head, which is the most divine part. (*Timaeus* 90a, 45d.) The mortal soul, which resides in the breast, was placed away from the immortal soul in order to avoid polluting the divine any more than was necessary. According to Plato, the mortal soul has two parts, one superior and one inferior. Plato here explains that the body is organized just as the women's and men's quarters are divided in a house. The superior part of the mortal soul, "which is endowed with courage and passion and loves contention, they [the gods] settled nearer the head . . . in order that being obedient to the rule of reason it might join with it in controlling and restraining the desires." (*Timaeus* 70a.) The inferior part of the mortal soul, that part which desires meat and drink and sex, was placed between the midriff and the boundary of the navel. It is the superior part of the mortal soul that Plato associates with the men's quarters, for it is men, not women, whom Plato views as capable of courage. Women are thus associated with the bodily desires, the part of the soul that Plato claims "would not comprehend reason, and even if attaining to some degree of perception would never naturally care for rational notions." (*Timaeus* 71a.)

This tripartite division and hierarchization of the soul into *logistikon*, the rational element, *thumos*, spirit, and *epithymia*, the appetitive element, is a theme central to Plato's philosophy. On the basis of it, he not only defined individual justice but also modeled the ideal state. Only when reason, aided by spirit, ruled the appetite would an individual achieve the harmony Plato called justice. Such a model also applied to the state. In the *Republic* Plato argued that the just state would be achieved only when those whose powers of reasoning were the strongest ruled. An understanding of this part of Plato's philosophy is essential for a full comprehension of Plato's perception of woman's role within the *polis*.

Plato advanced a philosophy of natural classes in which different classes of people would have different natures. These natures paralleled the divisions of the soul. The guardian class would consist of those whose powers of reason were strong enough to rule over the multitudes. The guardians would be assisted by a second class, the soldiers, representing spirit—those people possessed of courage and passion who loved contention. The multitudes, the artisans and producers, represent the appetite. In addition to these three classes would be slaves, a group Plato viewed as barely human. The ideal state is that in which people perform those functions for which their natures are best suited, and in which the guardians, assisted by the soldiers, rule. According to Plato, "the having and doing of one's own and what belongs to oneself [i.e. performing those functions for which one's nature is best suited] would admittedly be justice." (*Republic* 434a.) And just as the loss of control of the appetites brings about individual degeneration, a lack of harmony between those suited to rule and those by nature designed to be ruled leads to the ruin of the state.

But when, I fancy, one who is by nature an artisan or some kind of money-maker tempted and incited by wealth or command of votes or bodily strength or some similar advantage tries to enter into the class of the soldiers or one of the soldiers into the class of counselors and guardians, for which he is not fitted, and these interchange their tools and their honors or when the same man undertakes all these functions at once, then, I take it, you too believe that this kind of substitution and meddlesomeness is the ruin of a state. [*Republic* 434b.]

When we turn to Plato's views on women in the *Republic*, we find a position which appears to be in tension with his views in the *Timaeus*. Plato argues that bodily differences between women and men will not preclude women's inclusion within the guardian class. Since the guardians are those people who are self-ruled by reason, it appears that Plato is arguing for a form of equality between women and men that many have labeled feminist.[3] Prior to attempting to resolve this tension, we must look closely at Plato's reasons for including women within the guardian class.[4]

Taking as established the belief that each person ought to perform that function for which she or he is best suited by nature, Plato turns to the natures of women and men. Although acknowledging that their natures differ, Plato questions whether these differences are sufficient to entail that all women and men have different roles in the *polis*. Plato first points out that not all differences between people are relevant. For example, whether one is bald or long-haired is not indicative of a difference in nature. (*Republic* 454c.)

On the basis of this distinction, Plato argues that the simple fact of bodily differences between women and men, namely reproductive differences, is, in itself, not sufficient reason to conclude that the roles of women and men must differ. "But if it appears that they differ only in just this respect that the female bears and the male begets, we shall say that no proof has yet been produced that the woman differs from the man for our purposes, but we shall continue to think that our guardians and their wives ought to follow the same pursuits." (*Republic* 454d–e.)

The question, of course, here arises as to what counts as a relevant difference. Plato explains that the only relevant difference is that which is "pertinent to the pursuits themselves," and illustrates this by explaining that "a man and a woman who have a physician's mind have the same nature" but that "a man physician and a man carpenter have different natures." (*Republic* 454c–d.) In other words, bodily differences, such as hair length, are irrelevant. What counts are differences in the souls of individuals. Only those whose faculty of reason rules over the appetites are suited for the role of guardian. Thus, bodily differences, including sex, must be for Plato irrelevant.

On this basis, Plato argues that some women, those suited by their nature, will perform the function of the guardian, that is, be part of the ruling class. Given this, Plato advocates a similar education for girls and boys. "For the production of a female guardian, then, our education will not be one thing for men and another for women, especially since the nature which we hand over to it is the same." (*Republic* 456c–d.) Thus, some contemporary philosophers have argued that Plato's philosophy, although classist, was not sexist.*

Although, at first glance, the Plato of the *Timaeus* who argues that women are a secondary creation appears inconsistent with the Plato of the *Republic*, a closer look reveals an underlying continuity. First of all, it would be incorrect to think that because Plato includes women within the guardian class and argues that they are to receive a similar education, he believed in the equality of women and men. On the contrary, he held that women would be inferior to men in all things. (*Republic* 455c.) Just after making his point about the irrelevance of bodily differences, Plato makes a distinction between the gifted man and the man who is not so gifted. He explains that the gifted man learns easily, makes new discoveries on his own, and is served by his body in his rational pursuits, while the less gifted man learns only with difficulty, is unable to remember information, and is hindered in his intellectual pursuits by the needs of his body. He concludes this distinction by insisting that the masculine sex surpasses the female in all these traits. (*Republic* 455b–c.) In other words,

---

* Even apart from my forthcoming analysis, such a conclusion would be premature in that Plato discusses only the role of women in the guardian class. We do not know if he would advocate similar educations or roles within the other classes.

in all things women are less gifted than men. Although Plato included women within the guardian class, he did not think their capacities as rulers would be equal.

What is important to see in order to resolve the apparent tension between the account in the *Timaeus* and that of the *Republic* is that, without discounting gender differences, Plato viewed class differences as more relevant. Consistent with the *Timaeus*, Plato held that the souls of women would be inferior to those of men, but he qualified this a bit. The souls of some women, namely guardian women, would be superior to the souls of some men, namely those of the other classes. But within each class, it remained true that women would be inferior in ability to men. To fully understand Plato's views on women in the *Republic*, we must be clear on all the reasons why he included women within the guardian class. There is, of course, the point raised above, that Plato viewed bodily differences as irrelevant to an individual's nature. It is the nature of the soul, not the specifics of the body, that would determine one's function in society. Thus, precluding women from the role of guardian simply on the basis of bodily differences would have been inconsistent with Plato's overall philosophy.

But what of differences in the souls of women and men? Surely in the *Timaeus*, Plato has committed himself to the view that women are, in respect to their souls, inferior to men. In fact, given the creation myth in the *Timaeus*, we would expect women to be less capable of insuring the rule of the rational element over the appetite, whether it be at the individual level or that of the state. In the *Republic*, Plato does not deny this position, he simply modifies it. Guardian women, although superior in this respect to men of other classes, remain inferior to men of the guardian class. "The women and the men, then, have the same nature in respect to the guardianship of the state, save in so far as the one is weaker, the other stronger." (*Republic* 456a.) Furthermore, Plato actually did not hold that women's roles in the guardian class would be completely identical to those of men. Although agreeing that they "must take their part with the men in war and the other duties of civic guardianship and have no other occupation," he amends this by claiming that "in these very duties lighter tasks must be assigned to the women than to the men because of their weakness as a class." (*Republic* 457a–b.)

The importance of class differences comes in at this point. In the *Republic* Plato offers a eugenics program in which members of the guardian class, those by nature superior in soul to all other classes, would reproduce only with members of the same class. Plato explains that marriages must be arranged so that, as with hunting dogs or pedigreed cocks, the best would breed from the best, lest the class degenerate. (*Republic* 459a–b.) Furthermore, the best men are to cohabit with the best women, and more frequently than those who are less perfect. One of the "prizes" that Plato suggests conferring on young men of the guardian class who excel at their pursuits and thus prove their "metal" is "the opportunity of more frequent intercourse with the women." (*Republic* 460b; see also 468c.)

Given his belief in differences in the souls of people, and his implicit belief that these differences were hereditary, Plato quite consistently concludes that women of the guardian class should be raised and educated in the same way as the men of that class. Plato believed that such an educational program was necessary to identify which children would possess the requisite nature. Thus, the only way to determine which women were "the best of the breed" was to give them the type of upbringing that would insure the fullest development of their rational faculty. Plato's reasons for including women within the guardian class and insuring a similar education for women and men are hardly feminist.

Furthermore, although Plato downplays reproductive labor in the *Republic*, attention to this illustrates another reason why the roles of female guardians will be different from those of male guardians. Although Plato insures that the labors of nurturing and raising children will be delegated to women who are not guardians, the guardian women must bear children.* In fact, the best of the guardian women will bear the most children. "[T]he best men must cohabit with the best women . . . and on the young men, surely, who excel in war and other pursuits we must bestow honors and prizes, and, in particular, the opportunity of more frequent intercourse with the women, *which will at the same time be a plausible pretext for having them beget as many of the children as possible.*" (*Republic* 459d–460b, my emphasis.)† Plato insists that these women, "beginning at the age of twenty, shall bear for the state to the age of forty." (*Republic* 460e.) But the ages of twenty to thirty-five are exactly those times when the best of the guardians are to engage in studies enabling them to comprehend the power of dialectical reasoning, that reasoning ability necessary for attaining the position of ruler. (*Republic* 537b–540b.) Although the efforts of raising these children would be spared such women, they would still go through the physical exertions of pregnancy, birth, and lactation. Yet Plato viewed physical exertion as in tension with the labors of intense study. An instance of this is his rule that youths be released from gymnastics because physical exertion "incapacitates them for other occupations. For great fatigue and much sleep are the foes of study." (*Republic*

---

* The fact that Plato seems to assume that only women will take care of these children supports the suspicion that Plato would *not* advocate similar roles for free women and men in classes other than that of the guardian. Yet another reason for rejecting the label "feminist."

† Plato slips at this point, perhaps assuming, contrary to his own philosophy, that only men would excel at war. He does not mention prizes that would be given to women who excelled at war.

537b.) Thus, although not explicitly stated by Plato, it is fair to assume that he would have seen the exertions of reproduction as similarly limiting to women, especially for the best of the guardian women who were expected to bear many children for the state. Thus not only does Plato view women as less gifted than men, he would also perceive that those women who were most gifted would also be the most "incapacitated" by the exertion of reproductive labors during the years in which the most complex of the reasoning skills were to be achieved.* Given this, it is highly unlikely that Plato envisioned a guardian woman as actually ruling.

It is important to recognize that throughout the *Republic* Plato's concern is not directed at the rights or needs of the individual, but is aimed solely at the good of the state. He argues that there is to be no private home or family life amongst the guardians, for this could create a tension in the guardian-rulers between the needs of the state and their own personal needs. Thus to insure justice within the state, Plato demanded that guardians possess no "property, children, or kin."†

Plato is thus removing the distinction between the private and the public realm by politicizing marriage and reproduction. Marriages are to be arranged by the state. Children resulting from such unions are raised in common from birth, with every effort being made to insure that no woman or man recognizes her or his child. (*Republic* 460–461.) Plato's motive here is to make the good of the state the fundamental concern of all individuals by removing any possible tensions that could result from an individual's desiring the good of her or his family over that of the state. Thus, there is no realm, such as the home, that is reserved for women alone.

This interpretation—that is, that Plato's concern was for the good of the state rather than the rights of women—is further supported by his discussion of the state in the *Laws*. Plato here claims that in ordering a society, legislators must "devise a set of institutions for both sexes alike." (*Laws* 781c.) Although this sounds like contemporary pleas for "equal opportunity," Plato's intent here is radically different. His concern is rather that the failure to regulate the private realm, and women in particular, presents a potential threat to the state. He thus demands equal regulation, not because to do so is to treat women justly, but rather because failure to do so risks the good of the state.

* My position here is not that women are in fact so incapacitated by reproductive labors, but rather that Plato would have viewed them as such.

† It is revealing, and consistent with my claim that Plato views women as inferior to men in the *Republic*, to note the manner in which Plato refers to the nature of marriage in the ideal state. He speaks of the community of wives and children and claims that "women shall all be common to all these men." (*Republic* 464a, 457d.) He never speaks of men being in common to all the women. In other words, the relationship is not viewed as reciprocal.

It is a grave error in your law that the position of women has been left unregulated . . . the very half of the race which is *generally predisposed by its weakness to undue secrecy and craft*—the female sex—has been left to its disorders by the mistaken concession of the legislator. Through negligence of the sex you have then allowed many things to get out of hand which might be far better ordered than they are if only they had come under the laws. Woman—left without chastening restraint—is not, as you might fancy, merely half the problem; nay, she is a two-fold and more than a twofold problem, in proportion *as her native disposition is inferior to man's.* [*Laws* 780e–781b, my emphasis.]

Plato's assertion of equal laws and equal roles is thus quite consistent with his view of women as inferior to men. His concern is rather for public regulation of the private realm. As long as women are limited to the realm of family and the concerns of the family are deemed separate from those of the state, there remains a potential conflict of interests. "While the right regulation of the private households within a society is neglected, it is idle to expect the foundations of public law to be secure." (*Laws* 790b.)[5] Given that Plato viewed the "lust of procreation" as the most "imperious need and fiercest passion," the state will not be well-ordered as long as procreation is not within the public realm. In this way reason will rule over appetite. But the public regulation of procreation will occur only by making the private realm of family public, requiring public regulation of women as well as men.

Furthermore, it is important to notice that although Plato includes women within the guardian class, he rejects the "feminine"—roles or traits associated with emotions or nurturance. For example, no guardian, male or female, would participate in the rearing of children.[6] Thus we hear no mention of the guardians' developing nurturing qualities or the types of wisdom needed for the raising of small children. Essentially, guardians, both women and men, are to develop roles viewed as masculine within the Greek society: warriors, athletes, scholars, rulers. Women, then, can serve as guardians only to the extent that they are capable of being like men.

When the views of a philosopher concerning woman are looked at, as I have done here with Plato, the response is often raised that the philosopher's views on women simply reflect the misogyny of his culture—that is, that we cannot expect even the best of philosophers to rise above the prejudices of their society. The implication of such a response is that the misogynous views could simply be removed, leaving the philosophical system basically intact. Because of Plato's position on the feminine, we cannot dismiss his remarks on women so quickly. Even if we denied his assertion of woman's biological inferiority, we are still left with a systematic denigration of those traits and roles associated with the feminine in Greek society. Thus if we tried to correct Plato's gender bias simply by denying Plato's claim that women were not as capable as men, we would continue to perpetuate a privileging of the masculine over the feminine. We would, so to speak, be requiring that women be as capable as men in being "like a man." Plato's gender bias is not a tangential addition to his theory that can be simply excised. It is an integral part of his metaphysic.

Plato's discussion of woman involves the acceptance of the premise of woman's inferiority along with the denigration of traits associated with the feminine. Denying the importance of the bodily differences between the sexes, Plato posits differences in the souls of women and men. Woman's rational faculties are inferior to those of man, and thus she is more likely to act on the basis of her passions. As we will see in the next chapter, this belief in the relative weakness of woman's rational faculties became an accepted tenet within Western philosophy. However, Plato's cosmological explanation of this inferiority was replaced by the type of biological explanation found in the writings of Aristotle.

MUTILATED MEN: ARISTOTLE

Plato spends little time discussing the physical differences between women and men, arguing that what is significant is the nature of one's soul, not the configuration of one's body. Having made a distinction between soul and body, Plato argues that it is the soul that is essential, that is, it is the soul that *is* the person. Significant differences between women and men must then be attributable to differences in their souls, not in their bodies.[7]

Aristotle's position is in sharp contrast to Plato's. Aristotle argues that the soul is inseparable from its body, for form cannot exist apart from matter and the soul is the form of the body. (*On the Soul* II.1.) Thus, differences in the soul will be reflected in the body. Aristotle systematically examines the biological differences between the sexes, and ultimately associates differences in the natures of women and men with these biological differences.

A central premise of Aristotle's biology is that heat is the fundamental principle in the perfection of animals. Heat serves to "concoct" matter, that is, to enable it to develop. The more heat an animal is able to generate, the more developed it will be. "That which has by nature a smaller portion of heat is weaker." (*Generation of Animals* 726b 33.) An animal's degree of perfection is thus determined by the amount of heat it generates.

Aristotle argues that women generate less heat than men and thus concludes that woman is less perfect. His proof of woman's defect in heat is based upon a comparison of female and male "semen." Aristotle identifies the male ejaculate as semen and equates menses with male semen. Menstrual discharge "is analogous in females to the semen in males." (*Generation of*

Animals 727a 3–4.) The differences between male and female semen, so defined, are obvious: the male ejaculate is white in color and relatively sparse, the menses resemble blood and are, in comparison to the amount of the male ejaculate, profuse. Aristotle adds to this the tenet that semen is derived from the blood. From this he concludes that the differences between male and female semen are the result of the male's higher degree of heat.

Aristotle's argument goes as follows: Since the male ejaculate is derived from blood but does not resemble it, it has been transformed from its original state. A substance is transformed by being concocted, which is brought about by an infusion of heat. Thus the color and amount of male semen are the result of an infusion of heat that concentrates the potency and volume of the blood and turns it white. But the female semen is abundant and resembles blood. Thus, the appearance of female semen constitutes empirical proof that women are lacking in heat in comparison to men; that is, they do not have the heat needed to concentrate and concoct their semen. "It is necessary that the weaker animal also should have a residue greater in quantity and less concocted." (*Generation of Animals* 726b 30–31.)

A flaw in Aristotle's argument that is obvious from our contemporary vantage point is his equation of menses with female semen. Aristotle's justification of this equation was that "semen begins to appear in males and to be emitted at the same time of life that the menstrual flow begins in females" and that "in the decline of life the generative power fails in the one sex and the menstrual discharge in the other." (*Generation of Animals* 727a 5–10.) Since the menstrual flow, like the potency of the male ejaculate, commences at puberty and ceases with old age, Aristotle correctly concludes that it has to be associated with reproduction. His error is in equating it with male seminal fluids.[8]

Having thus "established" women's relative lack of heat, Aristotle employs it to account for a number of physiological differences between women and men. He claims, for example, that woman's defect in heat results in her being smaller and weaker than man. "The male is larger and longer-lived than the female . . . the female is less muscular and less compactly jointed, and more thin and delicate in the hair . . . more flaccid in texture of flesh, and more knock-kneed, and the shin-bones are thinner; and the feet are more delicate." (*History of Animals* 538a 23–538b 11.) But Aristotle was not simply chronicling differences between the bodies of women and men, he was evaluating women's differences as defects. Woman's "pallor and the absence of prominent blood-vessels is always most conspicuous, *and the deficient development of her body compared with a man's is obvious*." (*Generation of Animals* 727a 24–25, my emphasis.)

That Aristotle views woman's biological differences as defects rather than variations can be seen in his discussion of the original cause of woman's relative coldness. Aristotle argues that an embryo becomes female thus: "when the first principle does not bear sway and cannot concoct the nourishment through lack of heat nor bring it into its proper form, but is defeated in this respect, then must the material change into its opposite." (*Generation of Animals* 766a 17–21.) This statement reveals Aristotle's biases. We can see from it that he views the "proper form" of humans as male. In the Aristotelian teleological view of nature, nature always aims to create the most perfectly formed being—a male, given the previous bias. A female embryo, then, is the result of a lack or an incapacity, a deviation from the proper form.*

From this we can conclude that Aristotle viewed woman as, in a sense, a defective male—a being who, had the first principle held sway, would have developed into a man. "For the female is, as it were, a mutilated male. . . ." (*Generation of Animals* 737a 27–28.) This interpretation is further supported by Aristotle's discussion of literally mutilated males, eunuchs. Aristotle believes that his account is supported by the physical appearance of eunuchs, who as a result of their mutilation (removal of testicles) "depart so much from their original appearance and approximate closely to the female form." (*Generation of Animals* 766a 26–27.)

Because woman is not the "proper form" of a human, Aristotle labels her a "monstrosity."[9] Having defined a monstrosity as a "departure from type," Aristotle notes that the "first departure [from type] indeed is that the offspring should become female instead of male." (*Generation of Animals* 767b 8–9.) Aristotle immediately qualifies this by claiming that woman's departure from type is a "natural necessity." In other words, woman's defect in heat makes her unable to fully concoct her menstrual fluids, which are then available to provide the material out of which an embryo develops. The male, capable of concocting all of his matter, would have no residue with which to nourish a growing fetus. The monstrosity of woman is thus necessary for the reproduction of the species.

The evidence Aristotle offers in support of this explanation demonstrates the extent to which his biases affected his science.

Observed facts confirm what we have said. For more females are produced by the young and by those verging on old age than by those in the prime of life; in the

---

* Interestingly, Aristotle's view of man as the true form of humans is very similar to that of Plato, despite the fact that each has a very different explanation of the origin of the two sexes. For Plato, a woman is the result, via reincarnation, of a man who fails to control his appetites. For Aristotle, she is the result of a defect in the heat of the generative process. In both cases woman is the result of an inability or incapacity.

former the heat is not yet perfect, in the latter it is failing. And those of a moister and more feminine state of body are more wont to beget females, and a liquid semen causes this more than a thicker; now all these characteristics come of a deficiency in natural heat. [*Generation of Animals* 766b 28–33]

The belief that those individuals not in prime condition would be more likely to give birth to females is a logical conclusion of Aristotle's theory. Such individuals would be least able to provide the heat necessary for full concoction of a fetus into its "proper form." However, careful observations would have disconfirmed this hypothesis, since there is no correlation between the age of the pregnant woman or the man and the sex of their offspring.* Furthermore, the circularity of Aristotle's position is obvious from his claim that a "feminine" state of body results from a defect in natural heat.[10]

Although he argues that woman's "departure from type" is a natural necessity, Aristotle's perception of woman's differences is clearly negative. The terms he uses to describe woman and her differences have negative connotations: incapacity, deficiency, departure from type, mutilated male.

Like Plato's, Aristotle's metaphysics involves a notion of dichotomy. Characterizing the female as opposite to the male (*Generation of Animals* 766a 21), Aristotle defines this opposition as one of "contrariety." (*Metaphysics* 1958a 30.) According to Aristotle, every contrariety involves a privation, where a privation is an inability or incapacity that prevents a thing from becoming its opposite. (*Metaphysics* 1055b 15–20.) Obviously, for Aristotle the female is the privation of the male. The male is thus the measure of humanness, a measure against which the female is judged lacking. Aristotle describes the nature and function of the sexes through a series of opposed terms: capacity/incapacity, active/passive, form/matter. "The male and female are distinguished by a certain capacity and incapacity. (For the male is that which can concoct and form and discharge a semen carrying with it the principle of form . . . the first moving cause . . . the female is that which receives semen, but cannot form or discharge it.)" (*Generation of Animals* 765b 8–15.) "But the female, as female, is passive, and the male, as male, is active, and the principle of the movement comes from him." (*Generation of Animals* 729b 12–14.) "What the male contributes to generation is the form and the efficient cause, while the female contributes the material."

---

* I do not accept the view that Aristotle was an "armchair" biologist who merely speculated about living forms and did not base his conclusions on observational data. Many of Aristotle's tenets involved biological investigations and were not simply the result of accepting common opinion. If this example represents a lapse in Aristotle's critical empiricism, such a lapse would be significant, and would point to his bias of female biological inferiority.

(*Generation of Animals* 729a 9–11.) The female thus is inferior, the male superior.

Again, as the first efficient or moving cause, to which belong the definition and the form, is better and more divine in its nature than the material on which it works, it is better that the superior principle should be separated from the inferior. Therefore, wherever it is possible and so far as it is possible, the male is separated from the female. For the first principle of the movement, whereby that which comes into being is male, is better and more divine, and the female is the matter." [*Generation of Animals* 732a 3–8]

Since the soul is the form of the body, it is logical to expect Aristotle to posit differences in woman's nature as well as her body. The female form corresponds with the female psychology: Woman is "more compassionate than man, more easily moved to tears, at the same time is more jealous, more querulous, more apt to scold and to strike. She is, furthermore, more prone to despondency and less hopeful than the man, more void of shame, more false of speech, more deceptive, and of more retentive memory. She is also more wakeful, more shrinking, more difficult to rouse to action, and requires a smaller quantity of nutriment." (*History of Animals* 608b 9–13.)

Aristotle makes such association of nature and character clear in his *Physiognomonics*. For example, he discusses types of bodies found among brave animals and concludes that women's bodies evince numerous physical traits corresponding to a soft and cowardly character, including small heads, narrow visage, thin necks, weak chests, small sides, full hips and thighs, knock-knees, and small feet. (809b 3–10.) Thus woman's weakness of character is reflected in her body, so much so that Aristotle concludes that "the male is more upright and courageous and, in short, altogether better than the female." (814a 8–9.)

Woman's deficiency also affects her intellectual faculty. Aristotle divides the faculties of the soul into five parts. Listed in order of perfection from least to greatest, they are the nutritive, the sensitive, the appetitive, the motive, and the intellectual. Although he believed that all living beings have souls, Aristotle did not think that every being possessed all of these faculties. On his account, plants possess only the nutritive faculty, while the lower animals also have the sensitive and appetitive faculties. The higher animals additionally possess the motive faculty, but only humans possess all five faculties, including the intellectual. These faculties of the soul are ranked by Aristotle in terms of their "honor and dishonor" such that organisms possessing only the lesser faculties are less perfect. Not surprisingly, an animal's degree of heat determines which faculties she or he possesses. For example,

Aristotle explains that man's brain is the largest "because the heat in man's heart is purest" and concludes that man's "intellect shows how well he is tempered, for man is the wisest of animals." (*Generation of Animals* 744a 29–30.)

Given this association of heat and intellect, we would expect Aristotle to believe that in woman the highest faculty, the intellectual, is at best imperfectly developed. And this is exactly what we find. Concerning the intellectual faculty, Aristotle claims that "best of all are those whose blood is hot, and at the same time thin and clear. For such are suited alike for the development of courage and of intelligence. Accordingly, the upper parts are superior in these respects to the lower, the male superior to the female, and the right side to the left." (*Parts of Animals* 648a 9–14.) Woman's defect in heat, by affecting the temperature of her blood, thereby affects her intelligence. Woman possesses all the parts of the soul, but they are present in her in different degrees than in men.

It is important to realize that despite Aristotle's frequent sweeping generalizations such as the passage in *Physiognomonics* cited above, he did not believe that all men would be superior to all women. An individual's amount of heat is not the same for all men or for all women. For example, Aristotle argues that the inhabitants of warm regions will be more cowardly than those of cold areas. He believed that weather causes heat to escape from the body, thus cooling off the individual—with cool individuals being cowardly. Thus, Aristotle's theory, like Plato's, allows some women to be superior to some men, while inferior to others. This is exactly what we find. Aristotle makes a distinction between free men, free women, and slaves. Free women differ from free men in that their deliberative faculty is "without authority"; but they also differ from men (and women) who are natural slaves, for slaves possess no deliberative faculty at all. (*Politics* 1260a 12–14.) Thus, Aristotle is not making a simple correlation between gender and development; race* must also be factored in, for presumably, different races of people possess different levels of heat, which result in greater or lesser capacities for deliberation.[11]

Aristotle argues that the nature of woman's deliberative faculty requires that she be ruled by a man. A free woman is to be ruled by her husband. Aristotle employs the analogy of the rule "of the mind and the rational element over the passionate" to prove that the rule of a husband over his wife "is natural and expedient." Because "the male is by nature superior, and the female inferior . . . the one rules, and the other is ruled." (*Politics*

---

* The term "race" is not completely accurate. Aristotle believed that certain people were natural slaves, but this conviction was based on deficiencies in their intellectual faculties and did not correlate to skin color or other physical differences.

1254b 6–14.) Slave women also require the rule of a man, but in this case not the rule of a husband, but the rule of a master.* Aristotle associates women with the passionate element. A woman's reason, unlike that of a free man, does not hold authority over her passion. "It is surprising if a man is defeated by and cannot resist pleasures or pains which most men can hold out against, when this is not due to heredity or disease, like the softness that is hereditary with the kings of the Scythians, or that which distinguishes the female sex from the male." (*Nicomachean Ethics* 1150b 12–16.) Thus woman needs the guidance of one who can instruct her on proper action—her husband if she is free, her master if she is slave.

Since woman, whether slave or free, must of necessity be ruled, she is excluded from the realm of practical wisdom—reasoned arguments designed to identify right from wrong. "Practical wisdom is the only excellence peculiar to the ruler." (*Politics* 1277b 26–27.) Practical wisdom is the ability to deliberate about the good and to choose good acts. It is the capacity to apply knowledge of the good to particular situations. Woman, lacking this ability, is thus excluded from the realm of moral reasoning. Only the man of practical reason is capable of such excellence. "Excellence, then, is a state concerned with choice, lying in a mean relative to us, this being determined by reason and in the way in which a man of practical wisdom would determine it." (*Nicomachean Ethics* 1106b 36–1107a 2.)

It does not follow from this that women cannot be virtuous. In fact, according to Aristotle, a free woman becomes virtuous by placing herself in obedience to a virtuous man. Aristotle concludes that a free woman's virtue is different from that of a free man. "The temperance of a man and of a woman, or the courage and justice of a man and of a woman, are not, as Socrates maintained, the same; the courage of a man is shown in commanding, of a woman in obeying." (*Politics* 1260a 20–23.)

According to Aristotle, these differences in the functions and natures of the sexes are correlated with a division of labor within the households of free men and women. A woman is to bear and nurture children, be a companion to her husband, and preserve what he acquires. (*Politics* 1277b26.) Thus, Aristotle connects differences in the physiology of women and men not only to psychological differences but also to the social order. According to Aristotle, free women are by nature best suited for the private realm of family.

For nature has made the one sex stronger, the other weaker, that the latter through fear may be the more cautious, while the former by its courage is better able to ward

---

* The nature of the rule of a husband over a wife is to be constitutional; for a free woman, unlike a slave woman, possesses a deliberative faculty, but unlike her husband's, it is without authority. But the rule of a master over a slave, whether female or male, is to be despotic, for the slave has no deliberative faculty. See book I of the *Politics*.

off attacks; and that the one may acquire possessions outside the house, the other preserve those within. In the performance of work, she made one sex able to lead a sedentary life and not strong enough to endure exposure, the other less adapted for quiet pursuits but well constituted for outdoor activities; and in relation to offspring she has made both share in the procreation of children, but each render its peculiar service towards them, the woman by nurturing, the man by educating them. (*Economics* 1343b 29–1344a 8.)

Woman's excellences reflect her role in the family: "the excellences of the latter [woman] are, in body, beauty and stature; in soul, self-command and an industry that is not sordid." (*Rhetoric* 1361a 8–9.)

The fact that Aristotle marks out industry as an excellence of a free woman reflects woman's exclusion from the "higher" excellences, for Aristotle believes that leisure is required for their development. "In the state which is best governed and possesses men who are just absolutely, and not merely relatively to the principle of the constitution, the citizens must not lead the life of artisans or tradesmen, for such a life is ignoble and inimical to excellence. Neither must they be farmers, since leisure is necessary both for the development of excellence and the performance of political duties." (*Politics* 1328b 36–1329a 2.) The leisure required for the practice of excellence, which is in turn required for participation in government, will be bought for a few men by the industry of the women who are their wives and the women and men who are their slaves. In this way, all women support the state but are not fully a part of it.

Aristotle thus consistently develops an image of woman as lacking. Woman's generative deficiency in heat makes her unable to develop fully, resulting in a weakness of both body and character. Unable to control her passions, woman must be within the rule of man. Aristotle's position concerning woman's incapacity cannot be excised from his philosophy, leaving the broader system intact. It is not, for example, sufficient to correct his biology, simply removing the premise that woman results from a deficiency in heat. For Aristotle's tenet of woman's inferiority, his association of woman and the female with incapacity, passivity, and matter, is a fundamental part of his metaphysic. Although Aristotle might indeed have been "influenced by the misogyny of his time," he inscribed this misogyny into the very heart of his philosophy.

❧

Although Aristotle offers a bleaker image of woman than Plato, who grants that a few "superior" women are capable of developing the higher excellences, they share two central tenets:

1. the male as the true form of humankind
2. woman as deficient intellectually

Although neither Plato nor Aristotle see all males as fully human, since both perceive male slaves as lacking in the development of their higher faculties, still both see man as the original or proper form of humans. That is, although not all men in fact achieve full humanity, still *only* males are truly human. For Plato it is men who are the original race and it is the manly soul that is superior. In addition, as discussed earlier, Plato's theory of the just state involves the denigration of traits perceived as feminine. The manly soul, Plato tells us, carefully avoids all things associated with the female. For Aristotle, the female body is itself a mark of deficiency, that is, a deficiency in heat that defeats the first principle and results in a deviation from the proper form. The female, seen as the opposite of the male within the Aristotelian metaphysic, is thereby defined as originating from a privation, that is, an incapacity which prevents a thing from becoming its opposite. Although not all men achieve full humanity, only men are capable of it.

The second tenet concerns a specific deficiency, woman's intellectual incapacity. This tenet, like the first, will have profound implications for subsequent views on woman's abilities and proper role. Both Plato and Aristotle see woman as intellectually inferior to man.* Although they disagree on the origin of this inferiority—Plato attributing it to the soul, Aristotle associating it with a failure of the first principle which has an effect on both body and soul—they agree on its nature. For both philosophers, woman is less capable than man of developing the "higher" faculties, that is, rationality and morality.

In the following chapters I will trace the impact of this image of woman upon the history of Western philosophy. Turning first to the faculty of reason, I will in Chapter Three examine the views of philosophers who addressed the issue of woman's rational abilities, as well as examine the extent to which philosophical theories of rationality privilege "male" characteristics. In Chapter Four I will address the question of woman's moral abilities.

FURTHER READINGS

Primary Texts

PLATO
Republic, especially book V, 450–470
Timaeus, 41d–52e, 69b–70e, 76d–e, 90a–91d

---

* Although both make class or race distinctions, it nevertheless remains true that within each class, woman is inferior to man.

Laws, VI 780d–781d, 785b; VII 805d–807c; XII 944d–945b
Symposium, especially 201c–212c

ARISTOTLE
Generation of Animals, 716a 1–716b 15, 723a 20–732a 10, 736a 25–739b 35, 763b 20–767a 30
Politics, 1252a 25–1252b 15, 1253b 1–15, 1259a 35–1264b 25
History of Animals, 608a 30–608b 20
Economics, 1343a 15–20
Poetics, 1454a 15–25

Secondary Texts

PLATO AND WOMAN/THE FEMININE
Allen, Prudence. *The Concept of Woman: The Aristotelian Revolution 750 BC–AD 1250*. Montreal: Eden Press, 1985. Chapter I.
Bluestone, Natalie Harris. *Women and the Ideal Society: Plato's Republic and Modern Myths of Gender*. Amherst: The University of Massachusetts Press, 1987.
Coole, Diana H. *Women in Political Theory: From Ancient Misogyny to Contemporary Feminism*. Sussex: Wheatsheaf Books, 1988. Chapter 2.
duBois, Page. *Sowing the Body: Psychoanalysis and Ancient Representations of Women*. Chicago: The University of Chicago Press, 1988. Chapter 8.
Elshtain, Jean Bethke. *Public Man, Private Woman: Women in Social and Political Thought*. Princeton: Princeton University Press, 1981. Chapter 1.
Lange, Lynda. "The Function of Equal Education in Plato's *Republic* and *Laws*." In *The Sexism of Social and Political Theory: Women and Reproduction from Plato to Nietzsche*. Ed. Lorenne M. G. Clark and Lynda Lange. Toronto: University of Toronto Press, 1979. Pp. 3–15.
Lloyd, Genevieve. *The Man of Reason: "Male" and "Female" in Western Philosophy*. Minneapolis: University of Minnesota Press, 1984.
Martin, Jane Roland. *Reclaiming a Conversation: The Ideal of the Educated Woman*. New Haven: Yale University Press, 1985. Chapter 2.
Okin, Susan Moller. "Philosopher Queens and Private Wives: Plato on Women and the Family." *Philosophy and Public Affairs* 6, 4 (1977): 345–369.
———. *Women in Western Political Thought*. Princeton: Princeton University Press, 1979. Part I.
Saxonhouse, Arlene. *Women in the History of Political Thought: Ancient Greece to Machiavelli*. New York: Praeger, 1985. Chapter 3.
Spelman, Elizabeth. *Inessential Woman: Problems of Exclusion in Feminist Thought*. Boston: Beacon Press, 1988. Chapter 1.

ARISTOTLE AND WOMAN/THE FEMININE

Allen, Prudence. *The Concept of Woman: The Aristotelian Revolution 750 BC–AD 1250*. Montreal: Eden Press, 1985. Chapter II.

Brown, Wendy. *Manhood and Politics: A Feminist Reading in Political Theory*. Totowa, NJ: Rowman & Littlefield, 1988. Chapter 3.

Elshtain, Jean Bethke. *Public Man, Private Woman: Women in Social and Political Thought*. Princeton: Princeton University Press, 1981. Chapter 1.

Okin, Susan Moller. *Women in Western Political Thought*. Princeton University Press, 1979. Part II.

Saxonhouse, Arlene. *Women in the History of Political Thought: Ancient Greece to Machiavelli*. New York: Prager, 1985. Chapter 4.

Spelman, Elizabeth. *Inessential Woman: Problems of Exclusion in Feminist Thought*. Boston: Beacon Press, 1988. Chapter 2.

WOMEN IN CLASSICAL GREECE

Cantrella, Eva. *Pandora's Daughters: The Role and Status of Women in Greek and Roman Antiquity*. Trans. Maureen B. Fant. Baltimore: Johns Hopkins University Press, 1987.

Clark, Gillian. *Women in the Ancient World*. London: Oxford University Press, 1989.

duBois, Page. *Centaurs and Amazons: Women and the Pre-history of the Great Chain of Being*. Ann Arbor: University of Michigan Press, 1982.

Lefkowitz, Mary R., and Maureen B. Fant. *Women's Life in Greece and Rome*. Baltimore: Johns Hopkins University Press, 1982.

Peradotto, John, and J. P. Sullivan, eds. *Women in the Ancient World: The Arethusa Papers*. Albany: State University of New York Press, 1984.

Pomeroy, Sarah B. *Goddesses, Whores, Wives, and Slaves: Women in Classical Antiquity*. New York: Schocken Books, 1975.

CHAPTER THREE

THE MALENESS OF REASON

In the *Theaetetus* Plato depicts Socrates comparing himself to a midwife, boasting that his performance is superior to hers for to him alone is reserved the noble task of discerning the real from the unreal. "My patients are men, not women, and my concern is not with the body but with the soul that is in travail of birth. And the highest point of my art is the power to prove by every test whether the offspring of a young man's thought is a false phantom or instinct with life and truth" (150b–c).

The Platonic metaphor of the philosopher as midwife at once appropriates a female power and excludes women from its realm.[1] The act of reproduction is here reinscribed upon a male site. Both midwife and patient are men; women are erased. The philosopher-midwife deals only with the soul; the body, and all that is female, is transcended. Only truth, the offspring of the philosopher, is truly laudable.

The history of philosophy testifies to the prevalence of the image of reason as the bearer of truth. The privileging of reason and rationality is evident in the frequency with which they are among the criteria evoked to define what is uniquely and essentially human. The exclusion of women by the Platonic midwife metaphor raises the question of whether women are similarly excluded from the philosophical goal of the rational life. In other words, is rationality male?[2]

This question has many facets. At the surface is the question of whether women are depicted as incapable or less capable of being rational. Philosophers as well as scientists have examined everything from the size of women's brains to their role as mothers in an attempt to answer this question.* But

---

* Aristotle, for example, referred to differences in the lines of junction of the bones of women's and men's skulls to prove that men have larger brains and more developed intellectual capacities, while Rousseau, as we will see, reflected upon the effects of woman's role as wife and mother.

the question as to the maleness of reason and rationality is far more complex. To answer it, we must also consider the extent to which conceptions of rationality privilege traits historically associated with masculinity.* Given the widespread acceptance of the view that rational abilities are what make humans distinct and superior to other animals, any such association of rationality with traits considered masculine would involve a corresponding view of feminine characteristics and abilities as at best inferior to the rational faculties, and, at worst, irrational. Thus, to answer the question, we must consider the extent to which the attainment of rationality has been perceived as involving the control or transcendence of attributes historically identified as female— the body, the emotions, the passions, the appetites, sensuousness.[3]

To address the question of the maleness of reason, I shall examine the philosophies of René Descartes (1596–1650) and Jean-Jacques Rousseau (1712–1788).[4] Their conceptions of rationality are similar in that both associate traits viewed as masculine with reason. They differ, however, in their response to the feminine.

As I argued in the previous chapter, both Plato and Aristotle viewed women as more influenced by the passions than men. Aristotle perceived woman's physiology, in particular her reproductive role, as accounting for her emotionality: her jealousies, her deceptions, her despondencies, her whinings.[5] Plato similarly viewed women as more influenced by the appetites and passions than men, but believed that it was a woman's soul, not her body, that accounted for this. This association of women with the emotions and the appetites remained a consistent tenet of Western philosophical, religious, and scientific views of women.

Given the prevalence of this association of woman and the feminine with the emotions and the appetites, a crucial issue in an investigation of the maleness of reason is the relationship between rationality and these "feminine" traits. If, for example, the emotions are included within the realm of the rational and seen as providing an important source of knowledge, one might expect to find theorists positing women not only as capable of rationality, but perhaps superior in any of the areas of rationality which rely more upon emotions than on reason. In the second half of this chapter, I will examine a theory which offers such a conception of rationality, that of Jean-Jacques Rousseau. However, if the emotional is perceived as antithetical to the rational, that is, if the conception of the rational excludes those things historically considered female, then the relationship of women to the rational is far more problematic. The Cartesian conception of rationality, which com-

---

* To say that a trait is associated with masculinity does not mean that all men will be seen as equally possessing such a trait. In fact, men perceived to be inferior because of race or class have often been perceived as not fully masculine.

pletely excludes the emotions from the realm of the rational, provides an excellent basis for consideration of this latter relationship.

THE OPPOSITION OF REASON AND EMOTION: DESCARTES

René Descartes, in his *Rules for the Direction of the Mind*, offers a method that he believes will lead to certain knowledge of the nature of the universe. He argues that such knowledge can be acquired by breaking down complex beliefs and experiences into their basic constitutive elements until one reaches what is simple and self-evident. Once these "simple natures" are uncovered, they must then "be scrutinized by a movement of thought which is continuous and nowhere interrupted."[6] Descartes claims that through careful employment of deduction it is possible to understand how these simple natures combine in order to make up complex objects. He concludes that "the whole of human knowledge consists in a distinct perception of the way in which those simple natures combine in order to build up other objects."[7] According to Descartes, this method is applicable to all realms of knowledge. "We must not fancy that one kind of knowledge is more obscure than another, since all knowledge is of the same nature throughout, and consists solely in combining what is self-evident."[8]

Descartes' rules are, in a sense, instructions for properly regulating or operating our minds—"certain and simple rules such that, if a man observes them accurately, he shall never assume what is false as true, and will never spend his mental efforts to no purpose, but will always gradually increase his knowledge and so arrive at a true understanding of all that does not surpass his powers."[9] It was Descartes' conviction that as long as investigators limited their reason to that which could be known clearly and followed their rational powers exclusively, they would obtain incontrovertible knowledge. There are two very important assumptions here, the first being that the logic of reason mirrors the structure of reality. The second is that clear and distinct ideas are a source of truth about the world. If either of these presuppositions is incorrect, then knowledge is not certain.

To guarantee or ground both of these beliefs, Descartes attempts to prove the existence of a divine being, God, who so structured both mind and the world. Through reason, then, we are in a sense like God, and possess the ability to achieve, within the realm of human understanding, a "god's-eye view." Thus, human knowledge is envisioned by Descartes as objective, that is, independent of human concerns or values. To insure this absolute objectivity of reason, Descartes makes a distinction between reason, which can be a source of certainty, on the one hand, and the "fluctuating testimony of the senses" and the "blundering constructions of imagination," on the other hand.[10] The senses and the imagination are excluded from the realm of reason because these faculties are subjective and thus, according to Descartes, only impede the quest for objectivity.

A crucial component of Descartes' conception of rationality is his radical separation of mind and matter. Noting the variability of the senses and the fluctuating bodily needs, Descartes believes that certainty can be assured only if its source is mental and has no connection to the bodily. Descartes describes his technique for transcending the body in his quest for certainty in the *Meditations*. "I shall now close my eyes, I shall stop my ears, I shall call away all my senses, I shall efface even from my thoughts all the images of corporeal things, or at least (for that is hardly possible) I shall esteem them as vain and false; and thus holding converse only with myself and considering my own nature, I shall try little by little to reach a better knowledge of and a more familiar acquaintanceship with myself."[11] To be rational, one must be detached from the needs, desires, and particularities of the body. Only those activities which, on Descartes' account, successfully achieve this are sources of true knowledge: science, mathematics, philosophy.

A long history of privileging the soul or mind over the body exists. I have shown that the philosophy of Plato as well as that of Aristotle contains the view that the soul is superior to the body and that exertion of the body impedes intense mental labor.* But Descartes' distinction differs in that he defines mind and body in terms of opposition; that is, he sees them as mutually exclusive. The body thus does not provide such a basis or beginning for knowledge as we see in Plato's *Symposium*, where the journey to understanding beauty as an eternal form begins with bodily sexual attractions.[12] For Descartes, the body is an impediment to knowledge. One begins the Cartesian journey to truth not through the body, but by learning to overcome it.

The Cartesian ideal not only separates mind and matter, it polarizes reason and emotion. It involves a rejection of the Platonic view of the soul as a composite consisting of superior and inferior parts or faculties: reason, passion, and appetites. According to Descartes, "There is within us but one soul, and this soul has not in itself any diversity of parts; the same part that is subject to sense impressions is rational, and all the soul's appetites are acts

---

* Aristotle insisted upon this tenet despite his view that the body and soul were inseparable. In his account of generation, for example, he argues that the contribution of the father is superior to that of the mother in that his semen carries the soul of the fetus, which is responsible for the form of the child. The mother contributes only the material upon which the male semen works. Holding to both of the above tenets, however, caused problems for Aristotle. If body and soul were in fact inseparable, how could he argue that the father contributed the soul while the mother contributed only the "body"? To resolve this problem, Aristotle claimed that we should not view the soul as actually present in the semen, but rather as potentially present. "It is plain therefore that semen both has soul, and is soul, potentially." (*Generation of Animals* 735a 8–9.)

of will. The error which has been committed in making it play the part of various personages, usually in opposition one to another, only proceeds from the fact that we have not properly distinguished its functions from those of the body, to which alone we must attribute every thing which can be observed in us that is opposed to reason."[13] In the Cartesian view, the soul or mind is an indivisible mental substance—a thing which thinks. By thus limiting the mind to cognitions, Descartes has excluded emotions from the realm of the mental. Emotions come to be seen as arising from the body. Descartes tells us that the passions of the soul—love, desire, despair, pride, anger, joy— "are caused, maintained, and fortified by some movement of the spirits."[14] Descartes sees what he calls the "animal spirits" as arising from the body. "The little filaments of our nerves are so distributed in all its parts, that on the occasion of the diverse movements which are there excited by sensible objects, they open in diverse ways the pores of the brain, which causes the animal spirits contained in these cavities to enter in diverse ways into the muscles, by which means they can move the members in all the different ways in which they are capable of being moved."[15] Thus in rejecting the body as a source of knowledge, emotion is also excluded from the realm of the rational, and rather is seen as a source of error. To gain truth, individuals must purify their thought of all distortions—perspectives, emotional attachments, biases. One must reject all prejudice, scrutinize all beliefs no matter how obvious, and overcome the distractions of the body.

Descartes thus equates rationality with reason, seeing reason as a restricted activity that applies only in the sciences and philosophy—in those areas that Descartes believed could be completely divorced from the particularities of the body. The notion of a practical reason that enables an individual to function within the world of daily concerns is rejected by Descartes. He does not even see such an activity as an inferior sort of rationality, but rather excludes it from the rational realm. Descartes does not condemn such activities as being worthless, and in fact admits that the senses are reliable guides to our well-being. But he remains adamant about excluding the senses and the passions from the realm of rationality, arguing that they should not be seen as sources of truth. He explains that nature

truly teaches me to flee from things which cause the sensation of pain, and seek after the things which communicate to me the sentiment of pleasure and so forth; but I do not see that beyond this it teaches me that from those diverse sense-perceptions we should ever form any conclusion regarding things outside of us, without having [carefully and maturely] mentally examined them beforehand. For it seems to me that it is mind alone, and not mind and body in conjunction, that is requisite to a knowledge of the truth in regard to such things.[16]

Descartes believes that the ability to be rational is difficult to attain and advocates careful discipline and training to anyone who wishes to attain it. While admitting that the training would be arduous, he insists that all people are capable of achieving rationality. "Even those who have the feeblest souls can acquire a very absolute dominion over all their passions if sufficient industry is applied in training and guiding them."[17] His rules were designed to provide guidelines for a course of training that would enable one to silence the demands and interests of the body, and to separate oneself from the human perspective and achieve a Cartesian "god-like" viewpoint.

It is important to note that Descartes did not perceive this new image of rationality as in any way excluding women. He insists that all people possess equally the light of reason. "The power of forming a good judgment and of distinguishing the true from the false, which is properly speaking what is called Good sense or Reason, is by nature equal in all men."[18] In other words, each of us is capable of objectivity as long as we are capable of avoiding all influences which are subjective—our inclinations, our point of view, our bodily needs. In fact his belief that all people possess the "natural light of reason" led him to argue that his method was possible for anyone, even a woman, to follow.[19] A woman, just like a man, through training and careful attention, is capable of learning to ignore her emotions, her appetites, and everything else relating to the body. It would thus appear, at first glance, that Descartes' "man" of reason is gender-neutral. If we look beyond the surface, however, we find that the rational person is male.

To achieve a life of reason, one must be able to transcend the desires and needs of the body. Furthermore, one must focus only on universal issues, completely ignoring anything that is particular and personal. The needs of the body must be suppressed by the mind. The emotions must be dominated by the will. But this definition of the rational person is in tension with the traditional view of woman as being more influenced by the body and the emotions than man. In fact woman is frequently defined by qualities which directly contradict Descartes' requirements for rationality. To take one such example, Philo characterizes the female as "material, passive, corporeal and sense-perceptible, while the male is active, rational, incorporeal and more akin to mind and thought."[20] Woman is perceived as lacking the strength of will Descartes posited as necessary for dominating the emotions, a position accepted by Aquinas who tells us that "since woman, as regards the body, has a weak temperament, the result is that for the most part, whatever she holds to, she holds to it weakly."[21] And given that the needs of her body are viewed as far stronger than those of man, woman will be seen as less capable of suppressing them, a tenet that fed the belief in the sixteenth and seventeenth century that women are prone to witchcraft: "All witchcraft comes from carnal lust, which is in women insatiable."[22]

Descartes' conception of the rational person is antithetical to this image of woman as tied to the body and ruled by its dictates. Descartes himself did not discuss contemporary theories of woman's nature or proper role, so we do not know his personal position. Still the majority of his readers would have unquestioningly accepted this view of woman. Women had for centuries prior to Descartes been seen, and would for centuries after be seen, as inescapably bound to the concerns of the body by her role in reproduction—her pregnancies, her lactations, her menses. Given this conception of woman's nature, even if one accepts Descartes' view that women had the same mental capacities as men, she or he will still conclude that the suppression of the body is a far more arduous task for a woman, and thus one in which she is less likely to succeed.

Not only does the body of woman so impede her; her social role also handicaps her. The vast majority of Western philosophers, theologians, and scientists writing both before and after Descartes have accepted the Aristotelian view of the natural role of "civilized" women as that of wife and mother. That is, women from the most privileged classes are seen as naturally destined for a role whose very nature will obstruct them from living a life of the mind. The arduous training and dedication of Descartes' rational man will be obstructed by the daily chores and responsibilities of nurturing children and running a household. The leisure necessary for the pursuit of reason is not available to a wife and mother. This point was well made by Princess Elizabeth of Bohemia, who corresponded with Descartes about his method. "The life I am constrained to lead does not allow me enough free time to acquire a habit of meditation in accordance with your rules. Sometimes the interests of my household, which I must not neglect, sometimes conversations and civilities I cannot eschew, so thoroughly deject this weak mind with annoyances or boredom that it remains, for a long time afterward, useless for anything else."[23]

Descartes' claim that the rational person must attend only to the universal and avoid the particular is especially inconsistent with the social image of woman as mother. In the realm of the family, woman is perceived as being sensitive to the particular needs of each child, offering to each the type of warmth and protection appropriate to her or his personality. This image of maternal care, and its necessary ties to the particular, the personal, and the emotional, stands in opposition to Descartes' image of the rational person.

The "uncivilized" woman—the woman who is a slave, or a serf, or a laborer, or from a "savage" race—is even more handicapped by her social role, as well as societal prejudices concerning her natural abilities. The grueling labors necessary for basic survival for women of these groups completely precludes the life of leisure Descartes prescribes. Princess Elizabeth found it difficult to find sufficient free time to acquire Descartes' habit of meditation, but a poor woman would find it impossible to do so. By factoring in class and race in this way, it becomes clear that Descartes' rational man is not only male, he is European and upper class.

In addition, Descartes depicts the man of reason as involved in a very active role. Those individuals striving to achieve a life of reason must engage in years of difficult training, learning to carefully control their mind and dominate their body. Having overcome the obstacles of the body and painstakingly honed the abilities of the mind, one then meticulously scrutinizes and dissects objects in the quest for knowledge. Descartes depicts the man of reason as a hero on a heroic quest for truth—a path fraught with many difficulties but offering rich rewards for the one who succeeds. This image conflicts with the image of woman as passive and as lacking courage, by nature more suited for the concerns of the private realm of family. "For nature has made the one sex stronger, the other weaker, that the latter through fear may be the more cautious, while the former by its courage is better able to ward off attacks; and that the one may acquire possessions outside the house, the other preserve those within."[24] Despite Descartes' protestations that women are capable of reason, the image he presents of the rational person —active, controlling, independent, transcendent—is in tension with the accepted image of woman, a conception Descartes was not concerned to actively undermine.

The man of reason is not gender-neutral.* Should a woman wish to pursue the rational life, she would have to deny all that is seen as female—attachment to individuals, private interests, maternal feelings. She would have to learn to be cool, dispassionate, impersonal, distant, detached. She would have to deny the many voices of her upbringing and culture whose definition of her would preclude her success in the arduous training required for the life of reason, for all the traits needed for this life are stereotypically masculine. Even the positive characteristics associated with the feminine, such as empathy, nurturance, and imagination, would have to be rejected, for they are relegated to the irrational in the Cartesian system. Descartes' sharp opposition of mind and body, reason and emotion, thus has the effect of masculinizing rationality. A woman who wishes to attain the rational life must put aside all that identifies her as female. She must become male.[25]

An interesting parallel exists between the philosophy of Plato and Descartes concerning women and rationality. As I illustrated in the previous chapter, Plato included women in the guardian class, the only class he per-

---

* Although my focus here has been on gender, it is also important to remember that the man of reason is also not race- or class-neutral.

ceived as capable of developed rational thought, only to the extent that they were capable of being like men, that is, developing roles and characteristics viewed as masculine within the Greek society. Descartes' philosophy implicitly contains a similar prescription. A woman's role as wife and mother is an impediment to the life of the mind. The woman striving for the Cartesian definition of a life of reason would do well to abandon this role. In fact, the life of a guardian woman as envisioned by Plato appears well suited for the Cartesian woman of reason.

Descartes' denigration of the feminine cannot simply be omitted from his epistemology, thereby making it hospitable to women. That is, we cannot simply revise his philosophy in order to remove the direct bias against the feminine and the indirect and unintentional exclusion of woman from the rational life. An exceptional woman could perhaps achieve the life advocated by Descartes, but only if she renounced all that defined her as woman within her culture. Descartes' epistemology thus provides an excellent illustration of the ways in which gender is inscribed upon the philosophical conception of rationality.

Despite Descartes' desire to disclose a method accessible to all, women and men alike, his radical opposition between mind and body, reason and emotion, can be seen as more limiting than the Aristotelian view of women as, at best, possessing a faculty of reasoning inferior to that of man. In the Aristotelian view one can argue that woman's activities in the family involve reason. Although Aristotle would see such reasoning as inferior to that of the philosopher or scientist or ruler, still it is a form of reason. But in the Cartesian view, although woman is capable of the same level of reason as man—a tenet Aristotle would reject—she can achieve reason only outside of her role in the family and only if she is properly trained. The woman who does not pursue Descartes' method is not employing reason; that is, she has not acquired the ability to reason. Descartes thus would not view the many activities and responsibilities associated with running a household and raising children as involving reason.[26] Not only are the cycles of a woman's body seen as causing her to be more emotional, imaginative, etc., her lack of training, should she pursue her traditional role, comes to be seen as perpetuating these characteristics.

A woman who wishes to follow Descartes' methods must reject her culturally prescribed roles, must see the skills and thought processes associated with those roles as devoid of reason, must discipline a body whose dictates she has been taught to see as far more demanding than those of man's, must overcome the societally dictated view of herself as passive, as weaker, as timid. She must renounce all those things that define her as female. She must become the man of reason.

THE MARRIAGE OF REASON AND EMOTION: ROUSSEAU

Writing a century after Descartes, Jean-Jacques Rousseau provides an alternative model of the relation between rationality and the emotions. He rejects the Cartesian view that the emotions are a source of error which should be transcended. Instead, Rousseau argues for a conception of rationality that involves a "marriage" of reason and emotion, believing that a good society will arise only through the correct employment of both faculties. Rousseau's basic tenet is that reason divorced from emotion and the sensations, as in the Cartesian view of rationality, is at best useless, at worst corrupting. It does not guide one to a good life or a just society, and it often leads to a self-centeredness that closes one off to the altruism Rousseau perceived as necessary for full membership in society.

According to Rousseau, reason that is not barren is based on sensation and is in harmony with one's feelings. Having repudiated the Cartesian view, Rousseau's conception of rationality is more compatible with a Platonic view of a proper harmony of the parts of the soul—reason, passion, sensation. In his treatise on education, *Emile*, Rousseau attempts to outline a course of education for young Emile that would be consistent with this conception of rationality. Rousseau rejects the type of arduous training of the mind recommended by Descartes to still the needs and desires of the body. Emile will live a life of virtue, Rousseau tells us, only if he listens to the voice of conscience, for its principles are "graven on every heart."[27] Emile's education must cultivate in him a harmony of reflection, sensation, and feeling, for "the acts of the conscience are not judgments but sentiments. Although all our ideas come from outside, the sentiments evaluating them are within us, and it is by them alone that we know the compatibility or incompatibility between us and the things we ought to seek or flee."[28]

Rousseau believes that the basic motivating force of man* is self-love, *amour de soi*,[29] the "source of our passions, the origin and the principle of all the others, the only one born with man and which never leaves him so long as he lives."[30] Self-love, when properly directed, leads to altruism through the recognition of the common interests and needs between individuals, where people recognize that their personal needs and desires are not in tension with those of others. Such love leads to virtue and the good society when it is governed properly, that is, through the harmonious marriage of reason and emotion. "Love of self is a natural feeling which leads every animal to look to its own preservation, and which, guided in man by reason

* I use the gender-specific term here because it is not obvious that this tenet holds for women.

and modified by compassion, creates humanity and virtue."[31] Emile must thus be educated so that his actions and desires arise out of such love.

Rousseau, like Descartes, makes a distinction between reason and emotion, but unlike Descartes, he includes emotions within the realm of the rational. Reason and emotion complement one another. Whereas Descartes perceives the emotions as antithetical to rational action, arguing that a rational action is based exclusively on reason and equating rationality with reason, Rousseau views a rational action as including the emotions, that is, as consisting of reason guided by emotion. While Descartes offers a conception of rationality that is male, Rousseau includes those faculties historically perceived as "feminine"—the passions, the senses, the emotions—within the realm of the rational. Thus it appears that Rousseau has provided an image of rationality that does not privilege traits associated with masculinity over those associated with femininity. Do women then fare better, at least in regard to the perception of their rational capacities, within a philosophy like that of Rousseau in which rationality is not construed as male?

To answer this question, it is helpful to understand Rousseau's attitude concerning the issue of the equality of the sexes. In *Emile*, Rousseau explicitly rejects the view of woman as a misbegotten man. He explains that each sex is perfect in its own way and maintains that any attempt either to categorize one sex as superior to the other or to demonstrate their equality is in error. "How vain are the disputes as to whether one of the two sexes is superior or whether they are equal—as though each, in fulfilling nature's ends according to its own particular purpose, were thereby less perfect than if it resembled the other more! In what they have in common, they are equal. Where they differ, they are not comparable. A perfect woman and a perfect man ought not to resemble each other in mind any more than in looks, and perfection is not susceptible of more or less."[32]

Rousseau rejects the Aristotelian view that woman is like man, only inferior, that is, that women possess the same faculties and characteristics as men, but that these faculties and characteristics are less developed. Rousseau replaces the Aristotelian view of woman as lacking with the view of woman and man as equally perfect but different. In other words, women possess *different* characteristics and faculties from men. According to Rousseau, the traits unique to women are neither better nor worse than those unique to men; rather, both are perfect in their own kind. Thus Rousseau appears to be rejecting the centuries-long tradition of positing man as the measure against which woman is to be judged and found wanting.

Interestingly, despite Rousseau's rejection of the Aristotelian view, his depiction of woman is surprisingly similar. Concerning the relation of the sexes, Rousseau tells us that man is active and strong while woman is passive and weak. Man must "will and be able; it suffices that the other [woman] put up little resistance."[33] Woman is "made to please and to be subjugated."[34] Women are more docile, more modest, more timid, more clever, more extreme in everything.[35] Women desire physical attractiveness. "Not satisfied with being pretty, they want people to think that they are pretty."[36] This leads to an interest in adornment which in turns results in the development of taste, woman's primary faculty for making judgments.

According to Rousseau, these differences are the natural result of woman's particular role—wife and mother. Woman's job is to nurture and educate her children. She, further, must provide the foundation that will allow a bond of love to develop between the children and their father, thereby maintaining the union of the family.[37] Women also serve as helpmeets, furnishing their husbands with a haven from the public world and inspiring them to develop their abilities.

Although Rousseau's description of woman is similar to that of Aristotle, he does not justify his view of woman's role through reference to biological differences between the sexes. Nor does he point to differences in the souls or minds of women and men to justify different roles. Rousseau's philosophy offers a third option for justifying gender roles. He argues that innate differences between the sexes do not dictate differential roles, but that sex roles are necessary for the good of the state and thus should be enforced.* Thus Rousseau's views concerning woman and man's proper roles and abilities cannot be simply excised from his philosophy, leaving his epistemology and his social and political theory intact. The differences between women and men, differences which I will argue place woman in a position inferior to man, are a consequence of Rousseau's social and political theory. To remove the sexism from Rousseau's thought, we would essentially have to revise his entire philosophy.

In his discussion of the lives of humans prior to civilization, what he calls "the state of nature," Rousseau mentions no differences in the lives of women and men, with the exception of the fact that women will bear and suckle children. He perceives this as a time which is presocial, that is, a time when each individual lives independently from all others. Rousseau depicts the human being in the state of nature as "wandering up and down the forests, without industry, without speech, and without home, an equal stranger to war and to all ties, neither standing in need of his fellow-creatures nor having any desire to hurt them."[38] Rousseau saw this independence as limited only by sexual needs and the needs of infants. As to sexual needs, "the sexes

* The mirror opposite of Rousseau is, of course, Plato, who argues that the good of the state requires prohibiting gender differences, at least among the guardian class. Still, Plato advanced this tenet while also embracing the position that a womanly soul is inferior to a manly soul. Presumably all guardian women would have manly souls. As I will discuss in Chapter Four, Kant adopts Rousseau's explanation to justify gender roles.

united without design, as accident, opportunity, or inclination brought them together . . . and they parted with the same indifference." A woman nursed her children, "but as soon as they were strong enough to go in search of their own food, they forsook her of their own accord."[39]

Rousseau attributes the origin of sex roles to the establishment of families. "The sexes, whose manner of life had been hitherto the same, began now to adopt different ways of living. The women became more sedentary, and accustomed themselves to mind the hut and their children, while the men went abroad in search of their common subsistence."[40] With the evolution of society, the family and woman's role in the family become useful. Rousseau believes that it is only through the family, that is, through a man's attachment to his children, that he will learn to love and support the state. He contends that a father's love of his children is "the principle of the love one owes the state . . . [it is] by means of the small fatherland which is the family that the heart attaches itself to the large one . . . [it is] the good son, the good husband, and the good father who make the good citizen!"[41]

Thus concluding that different social roles are necessary for the good of the state, Rousseau infers that the education of women must be different from that of men. Rousseau devotes the final chapter of his treatise on education to the education of women. He argues that a woman is to be educated to perform her duties, to "please men, to be useful to them, to make herself loved and honored by them, to raise them when young, to care for them when grown, to counsel them, to console them, to make their lives agreeable and sweet."[42] Such an education will insure that woman is different from man.[43] It will make her weaker by offering her far less training in physical endurance and strength than that given to man. Woman will be more docile because her education will constrain her more than will man's.

If we look carefully at Rousseau's image of the role for which a woman's education is to prepare her, we find that her entire life revolves around man. While obeying him, it is also her job to help and guide her husband. In order to be a guide to her husband, a woman must carefully manage his love. Rousseau admonishes each wife to make sure that she is "cherished by [her] favors and respected by [her] refusals."[44] In other words, Rousseau believes that a woman is to preserve the love of her husband by carefully regulating their sexual contact. By making her assents to sex "rare and precious," a woman retains her husband's heart and thus has the power over him she needs to guide him. Rousseau explains to Sophie, the woman educated to be the wife of Emile, that through such love Emile "will give you his confidence, listen to your opinions, consult you about this business, and decide nothing without deliberating with you about it. It is by this means that you can bring him back to wisdom when he goes astray; lead him by a gentle persuasion;

make yourself lovable in order to make yourself useful; and use coquetry in the interests of virtue and love to the benefit of reason."[45]

We find the beginning of an answer to the question concerning Rousseau's perception of woman's rational abilities in his discussion of the relation of the sexes. He argues that rationality requires a blend of reason and emotion. Investigating his views on gender roles, we find that he, like numerous philosophers before him, assigns to woman the realm of emotion. Woman serves as emotion or nature to man's reason. It is only in conjunction with emotion that reason leads to the good. Thus woman assists man by insuring that his reason is well balanced by emotion. Just as reason must rule emotion, while being guided by it, so too with the relation between the sexes. "In becoming your husband, Emile has become the head of the house. It is for you to obey, just as nature wanted it. However, when the woman resembles Sophie, it is good that the man be guided by her. This is yet another law of nature. And it is in order to give you as much authority over his heart as his sex gives him over your person that I have made you the arbiter of his pleasures."[46] While being subordinate to her husband, she is to provide emotional guidance.

Since Rousseau depicts rationality as involving a complex interdependence between reason and emotion, with woman affiliated with emotion and man with reason, can we then conclude that he has truly envisioned woman and man as different but equal in terms of rationality? Unfortunately we cannot. As promising as Rousseau's theory might appear, a careful examination of his writings reveals that he continues to privilege reason over emotion. Reason, according to Rousseau, selects from emotion that which is of value. Notice the difference in the relationship between reason and emotion: emotion *guides* reason, but reason *controls* emotion. There is in this a subtle privileging of reason over emotion despite Rousseau's insistence on complementarity. His discussion of the education of Emile exhibits this asymmetry:

We work in collaboration with nature, and while it forms the physical man, we try to form the moral man. But we do not make the same progress. The body is already robust and strong while the soul is still languorous and weak, and no matter what human art does, temperament always precedes reason. *Up to now we have given all our care to restraining the former and arousing the latter*, in order that man may as much as possible always be one. In developing his nature, we have sidetracked its nascent sensibility; *we have regulated it by cultivating reason. The intellectual objects moderated the impression of the objects of sense.* In going back to the principle of things we have protected him from the empire of the senses.[47]

When we look at the realms of knowledge available to women as compared to those of men, we find a parallel asymmetry in the relation of women and men to rationality. Women, on Rousseau's account, are incapable of many types of rationality. In his discussion of Sophie, Rousseau explains that the "art of thinking is not foreign to women, but they ought only to skim the sciences of reasoning. Sophie gets a conception of everything and does not remember very much. Her greatest progress is in ethics and in matters of taste. As for physics, she remembers only some idea of its general laws and of the cosmic system."[48] Rousseau excludes women from the sciences on the grounds that they are incapable of grasping general principles or generalizing ideas. "The quest for abstract and speculative truths, principles, and axioms in the sciences, for everything that tends to generalize ideas, is not within the competence of women."[49]

Rousseau depicts woman as capable only of what he called practical reason. Woman is good at getting things done, for she is skillful at finding the means for accomplishing a given end.[50] But she cannot determine or evaluate ends themselves, for she cannot grasp general principles. She achieves virtue not through reason, but by modesty. "While abandoning man to immoderate passions, He [God] joins reason to these passions in order to govern them. While abandoning woman to unlimited desires, He joins modesty to these desires in order to constrain them."[51] Emile's education is very different from Sophie's. He is carefully tutored in developing reason and doing so independent of authority. Rousseau stresses that Emile must be educated to make reliable judgments, for this ability is the necessary basis for morality. Since Rousseau privileges reason over emotion in his account of rationality, this difference in the education and roles of Sophie and Emile will result in Sophie being less capable of rationality than Emile.

Rousseau would protest that this simply means that woman's faculties are different from those of men, not inferior. To hold to this position, Rousseau must not treat the ability to generalize or determine ends as a higher or more valuable faculty. But in his discussion of the evolution of humans from the state of nature to the civil state, Rousseau does privilege man's abilities, seeing them as the result of a higher stage of development.

Rousseau believes that humans would follow their impulses and appetites in the state of nature. It is only in the civil state that man can listen to "the voice of duty" and substitute justice for instinct. Further, in the civil state, man is able to "consult his reason before heeding his inclinations."[52] Rousseau clearly depicts the civil state as superior to that of nature. "Although in this state he deprives himself of several advantages given him from nature, he gains such great ones, his faculties are exercised and developed, his ideas broadened, his feelings ennobled, and his whole soul elevated to such a point that . . . he ought ceaselessly to bless the happy moment that tore him away from it forever, and that changed him from a stupid, limited animal into an intelligent being and a man."[53]

But the very qualities that mark man's evolution out of the state of nature and keep him from being a stupid animal—substituting justice for instinct, acting on duty, listening to reason above inclinations—are the very characteristics that woman's role precludes. A woman cannot act upon duty or justice, for these abstract principles are beyond her comprehension. She cannot base her life on objective analysis rather than inclination, for her realm is that which pleases. Women act, not out of duty, but rather on the basis of taste. Despite his protests to the contrary, Rousseau provides a criterion for comparing the traits of women and men. On the basis of this criterion, it appears that women have not fully evolved.

This image of woman as less evolved is repeated in *Emile*:

Those who regard women as an imperfect man are doubtless wrong, but the external analogy is on their side. Up to the nubile age children of the two sexes have nothing apparent to distinguish them: the same visage, the same figure, the same complexion, the same voice. Everything is equal: girls are children, boys are children; the same name suffices for beings so much alike. Males whose ulterior sexual development is prevented maintain this similarity their whole lives; they are always big children. And women, since they never lose this same similarity, seem in many respects never to be anything else.[54]

Women like Sophie remain forever children, men like Emile evolve into adults. Sophie acts on the basis of taste, Emile develops conceptions of justice and duty as the basis for his actions. This hierarchizing of Emile's abilities over Sophie's, seeing the former as higher or more evolved, undercuts Rousseau's attempt to reject the view that woman's differences make her inferior to man.

This argument reveals that Rousseau did not intend Emile to represent mankind in general, but only "civilized" man. For just as Rousseau depicts woman as incapable of participation in the civil state, so too, Rousseau saw whole races of people as what he called "savage," that is, as having yet to evolve from a state of nature to the civil state. He refers, for example, to "the Caribbeans, who have as yet least of all deviated from the state of nature."[55] Despite Rousseau's romanticization of the life of the "savage," his biases are clearly in favor of civilized man, whose sacrifices in leaving a state of nature are well compensated by the benefits of the civil state—the broadened ideas, ennobled feelings, and elevated souls. Just as Emile represents only civilized man, Sophie portrays civilized woman, who does not seem to be equally well compensated by the benefits of the civil state.

This asymmetry in the relation of civilized women and men to rationality is further highlighted by the fact that woman's realm of competence does not have knowledge as its end, but rather the satisfaction of the needs of man.

Speaking now only of the civilized woman, Rousseau tells us that woman's rationality is directed at man—to manipulate him into doing what she wants as well as to fulfill his desires. "Woman, who is weak and who sees nothing outside the house, estimates and judges the forces she can put to work to make up for her weakness, and those forces are men's passions."[56] Woman's area of study is to be "the mind of man." Rousseau is not here encouraging woman to pursue a study of psychology. He makes it clear that a woman will not be interested in the nature of the human mind in general, but only in the minds of those men with whom she shares her life. Woman's rationality, then, consists of the ability to "penetrate their [her husband's and her father's] sentiments by their words, their actions, their looks, their gestures. She must know how to communicate to them—by her words, her actions, her looks, her gestures—the sentiments that she wishes to communicate without appearing even to dream of it."[57] Civilized woman's entire education, her entire being, is thus directed at man.

The civilized man is able to understand the laws of the universe and to establish and govern a just state. The civilized woman's "science" is the ability to see what is going on in men's hearts. Her rationality is defined in terms of man, that is, in terms of man's needs. Man's rationality, although at times guided by woman, is of a realm independent of her. Rousseau tells us that "man says what he knows, woman says what pleases."[58] But her primary concern is with what is pleasing to man, while man's knowledge is of the just state, of science, of morality. In this sense, man's rationality is not dependent on woman, while woman's rationality is inherently dependent on man. The subject of her knowledge is man. Without man, woman would possess no knowledge. Without woman, man's knowledge would not be as well guided, but it would still exist.

Just as there is an asymmetry in the interdependence of reason and emotion, so too is there one between woman and man. Although men depend on women, women's dependence is greater. "Woman and man are made for one another, but their mutual dependence is not equal. Men depend on women because of their desires; women depend on men because of both their desires and their needs. We would survive more easily without them than they would without us."[59] The characteristics of woman, if properly directed, address the needs of man. "Woman is made specially to please man. If man ought to please her in turn, it is due to a less direct necessity."[60] Women fulfill their role in the civil state by adapting themselves to men. Sophie is to be educated to understand and respond to the needs of Emile. But Emile's education is independent of Sophie. True, he will be inspired by her. Sophie causes Emile to truly experience passion. But it is up to Emile to "rule it like a man."[61] Woman's entire life is directed to pleasing and guiding her husband, while being a husband and ruling his wife is only one of man's roles.

A civilized woman's education is aimed at fitting her to man. Although Rousseau claims that woman and man are to complement one another, he never discusses directing man's education to fit him to woman. Sophie is educated to be the perfect wife to Emile. Emile is educated to be the ideal man. Evoking the grandeur and victories of Sparta, Rome, and the ancient Germans, Rousseau explains that good women inspire men to glory and virtue.[62] But we are never told how a good man inspires his wife. Emile's education, described in detail in four chapters, is never directed at responding to the needs of Sophie. Sophie, whose education is discussed in one chapter, is an addition. "After having tried to form the natural man, let us also see how the woman who suits this man ought to be formed so that our work will not be left imperfect."[63] For Rousseau, Emile's life would lack something without Sophie, but Sophie's life would be completely purposeless without Emile—a clear asymmetry. Furthermore, woman's happiness is completely dependent on the happiness of her husband. "Every man who is pleased in his home loves his wife. Remember that if your husband lives happily at home, you will be a happy woman."[64] Without a wife, a man's happiness may not be complete, but without a husband, a woman has no happiness. The asymmetry is transparent.

An additional sign of this asymmetry is the fact that Rousseau depicts woman in the civil state as limited to the private realm of family, while the civilized man has a role in both the private and public realms. Emile must enter not only into the private realm as head of the family but also into public social life. Sophie is important only insofar as she serves to assist Emile in these two functions. That is, she provides the conditions necessary for Emile to have access to both the private and public realms. While man lives between the two realms, woman is confined to the private realm and has no direct access to the public. Rousseau is adamant concerning women's participation in the public realm. He argues that any direct participation by women would undermine the body politic.[65] The political realm is a masculine realm. Women ought to participate in it only very indirectly, since their connections to individuals would hinder or preclude their participation in what Rousseau calls "the general will," which he sees as necessary for participation in the public realm, especially the making of laws. Like Plato, Rousseau views woman's attachment to the family and the particular as a danger to the functioning of the state. The general will, Rousseau explains, must transcend the particular needs of the family and focus on the common good. Sophie will see only the needs of her family, and thus her concerns will be in tension with those of the state. Unlike Plato, Rousseau seeks to solve the problem by carefully confining women to the private realm, making their access to the public realm limited to the extent to which they could influence their husbands.

Despite Rousseau's protests of complementarity, woman's differences function to reinforce man's identity. Her identity is secondary and contingent. Woman functions, in Rousseau's account, to reinforce maleness and the masculine public realm. Woman has an identity only derivatively. She is not capable of the autonomy Rousseau so highly esteems and perceives as necessary for society.[66] The type of rationality of which civilized woman is capable has only instrumental value, serving to assist man and guide his reason.

The models of rationality provided by Descartes and Rousseau stand in sharp contrast concerning the relation between reason and emotion. Descartes' theory denigrates the emotions, placing them in the realm of the irrational, while Rousseau develops a theory of rationality which involves a marriage of reason and emotion, viewing emotion as reason's guide. When the gender implications of these two models are examined, we find that both alternatives are fraught with problems.

The Cartesian system appears to provide a gender-neutral image of rationality—a model applicable to all people. However, when the model is examined carefully, we find that the traits associated with rationality correlate with traits historically considered masculine, while the traits associated with irrationality correspond to characteristics viewed as feminine and attributed to women. Given Western conceptions of gender identity, cultural expectations concerning woman's nature, and social institutions such as marriage and family which place women in the role of wife and mother as traditionally defined, such a model of rationality will subtly exclude women from the rational life. We thus see that a model of rationality that privileges traits viewed as masculine cannot be truly gender-neutral, despite protests that it is open to women as well as to men.

There is thus a complex interdependence between the philosophical conception of rationality and the social and cultural institutions at play in any historical time period. If such institutions define certain traits as masculine and associate them with men, then any conception of rationality which emphasizes such traits will be gender-specific. Despite Descartes' willingness to include women in the life of the mind, his defining terms exclude them.

Rousseau, in contrast to Descartes, did not exclude faculties associated with women from the rational realm. In arguing for a harmony of reason and emotion, Rousseau appears to have offered a conception of rationality that does not privilege masculine traits. Thus, in Rousseau's conception, the rational life does not require the suppression of the emotions, a faculty historically associated with women. Achieving rationality does not require transcending feminine characteristics.

However, Rousseau, like Descartes, perpetuates the distinction between reason and the emotions. Although he argues that knowledge is obtained only through the interaction of the two faculties, they remain separate and distinct faculties with reason valued over emotion. Furthermore, while denying a biological origin for gender differences, Rousseau advocates roles for women and men that would perpetuate the greater association of the emotions with women and reason with men while at the same time seeing reason as superior to emotion. Rousseau's attempt to argue for the thesis of "different but in their own way perfect" concerning the nature of the sexes is undercut by the fact that he privileges men's abilities and roles over those of women, making man's activities primary and independent and woman's activities and abilities secondary and dependent.

We thus learn a number of important lessons from an examination of gender in Descartes and Rousseau's theories of rationality. From Descartes we discover that an attempt to offer a nonsexist model of rationality of which women and men are equally capable will be unsuccessful if the abilities and faculties constituting rationality are said to be made up of traits perceived as masculine and to exclude traits accepted as feminine. Nor will it do to simply reverse this ordering and stress traits perceived as feminine and exclude traits accepted as masculine.* A truly nonsexist model of rationality either must include a mixture of feminine and masculine traits with no privileging of either gender or must occur in a social context in which the concepts of masculine and feminine do not exist. As we learned from Rousseau, replacing the Cartesian model of rationality with a model that includes a mixture of feminine and masculine qualities is not sufficient to insure a nonsexist model of rationality. Rousseau's subtle ranking of masculine traits over feminine led to an image of rationality as a male endeavor despite his emphasis on the harmony of reason and emotion. Rousseau also teaches us that a model of rationality that posits different but complementary cognitive abilities for the sexes can be nonsexist only if there is no attempt to privilege the traits or abilities assigned to one sex over those of the other. In other words, the ways in which these abilities are different must carry no connotation of inferiority or lack.

Both Rousseau and Descartes perpetuated the view of the male as the "true form." This tenet, elaborated by both Plato and Aristotle, is found in their philosophy through their unquestioned privileging of qualities historically viewed as masculine. I now turn to the question of the extent to which this tenet affected theories of morality.

---

* Similar lessons can be inferred from this analysis concerning nonracist and nonclassist models of rationality. That is, such models of rationality must not privilege traits associated with one race or class over those associated with another.

FURTHER READINGS

Primary Texts

DESCARTES
Meditations on First Philosophy, especially meditations III and IV
Passions of the Soul, especially articles XXVII, XXXIII, XLVII, and L
Rules for the Direction of the Mind, especially rules III, IV, VII, and XII

ROUSSEAU
"A Discourse on the Origin of Inequality," especially pp. 214–240 (in *The Social Contract*, trans. G. D. H. Cole [New York: E. P. Dutton and Company, 1950])
Emile, or On Education book V

Secondary Texts

DESCARTES AND WOMAN/THE FEMININE
Bordo, Susan. *The Flight to Objectivity: Essays on Cartesianism and Culture.* Albany: State University of New York Press, 1987.
Lloyd, Genevieve. *The Man of Reason: "Male" and "Female" in Western Philosophy*. Minneapolis: University of Minnesota Press, 1984. Chapter 3.
Thompson, Janna. "Women and the High Priests of Reason." *Radical Philosophy* 34 (1983): 10–14.

ROUSSEAU AND WOMAN/THE FEMININE
Coole, Diana H. *Women in Political Theory: From Ancient Misogyny to Contemporary Feminism*. Sussex: Wheatsheaf Books, 1988. Chapter 5.
Elshtain, Jean Bethke. *Public Man, Private Woman: Women in Social and Political Thought*. Princeton: Princeton University Press, 1981. Chapter 4.
Kennedy, Ellen, and Susan Mendus, eds., *Women in Western Political Philosophy: Kant to Nietzsche*. New York: St. Martin's Press, 1987.
Lange, Lynda. "Rousseau and Modern Feminism." *Social Theory and Practice* 7 (1981): 245–277.
———. "Rousseau: Women and the General Will." In *The Sexism of Social and Political Theory: Women and Reproduction from Plato to Nietzsche*. Ed. Lorenne M. G. Clark and Lynda Lange. Toronto: University of Toronto Press, 1979.
Lloyd, Genevieve. *The Man of Reason: "Male" and "Female" in Western Philosophy*. Minneapolis: University of Minnesota Press, 1984. Chapter 4.
———. "Rousseau on Reason, Nature and Women." *Metaphilosophy* 14, 3 and 4 (1983): 308–326.

Martin, Jane Roland. *Reclaiming a Conversation: The Ideal of the Educated Woman*. New Haven: Yale University Press, 1985. Chapter 3.

Okin, Susan Moller. *Women in Western Political Thought*. Princeton: Princeton University Press, 1979. Part III.

Schwartz, Joel. *The Sexual Politics of Jean-Jacques Rousseau*. Chicago: University of Chicago Press, 1984.

Weiss, Penny A. "Rousseau, Antifeminism, and Woman's Nature." *Political Theory* 15, 1 (1987): 81–98.

Weiss, Penny, and Anne Harper. "Rousseau's Political Defense of the Sex-Roled Family." *Hypatia: A Journal of Feminist Philosophy* 5, 3 (1990): 90–109.

WOMAN AND RATIONALITY

Aiken, Susan Hardy, et al., eds. *Changing Our Minds: Feminist Transformations of Knowledge*. Albany: State University of New York Press, 1988.

Code, Lorraine. *What Can She Know? Feminist Theory and the Construction of Knowledge*. Ithaca: Cornell University Press, 1991.

Collins, Patricia Hill. *Black Feminist Thought*. Winchester, MA: Unwin Hyman, 1990.

Duran, Jane. *Toward a Feminist Epistemology*. Savage, MD: Rowman & Littlefield, 1991.

Gergen, Mary McCanney, ed. *Feminist Thought and the Structure of Knowledge*. New York: New York University Press, 1988.

Harding, Sandra. *Whose Science? Whose Knowledge?* Ithaca: Cornell University Press, 1991.

Hekman, Susan J. *Gender and Knowledge: Elements of a Postmodern Feminism*. Boston: Northeastern University Press, 1990.

Jaggar, Alison M., and Susan R. Bordo, eds. *Gender/Body/Knowledge: Feminist Reconstructions of Being and Knowing*. New Brunswick. Rutgers University Press, 1989.

Keller, Evelyn Fox. *Reflections on Gender and Science*. New Haven: Yale University Press, 1985.

Levesque-Lopman, Louise. *Claiming Reality: Phenomenology and Women's Experience*. Totowa: Rowman & Littlefield, 1988.

Nelson, Lynn Hankinson. *Who Knows: From Quine to a Feminist Empiricism*. Philadelphia: Temple University Press, 1990.

WOMEN IN SEVENTEENTH- AND EIGHTEENTH-CENTURY FRANCE

Gibson, Wendy. *Women in Seventeenth-Century France*. Basingstoke: Macmillan, 1989.

Jacobs, Eva, ed. *Women and Society in Eighteenth-Century France*. London: Athlone Press, 1979.

Landes, Joan B. *Women and the Public Sphere in the Age of the French Revolution*. Ithaca: Cornell University Press, 1988.

Lougee, Carolyn C. *Le paradis de femmes: Women, Salons, and Social Stratification in Seventeenth-Century France*. Princeton: Princeton University Press, 1976.

Spencer, Samia, ed. *French Women and the Age of Enlightenment*. Bloomington: Indiana University Press, 1984.

CHAPTER FOUR

(A)MORAL WOMAN

The Cartesian view of rationality, with its privileging of masculine characteristics, has gone hand in hand with a conception of morality which
posits reason as the sole or primary source of moral action.* Accepting the
Cartesian opposition of reason and emotion, one argues that an action is
moral only if it is based solely on reason. Emotions, seen as transitory and
capricious, are rejected as a source of knowledge of the good or of the just.
In other words, individuals act morally only if they abstract themselves from
their inclinations and desires and base their actions on reason. Moral principles
are seen as universal, that is, valid for all individuals and knowable by any
rational moral agent. This conception of morality has given birth to numerous
schools of thought concerning the nature of good. Utilitarians, for example,
have argued that the worth of an action is determined by its effects, while
deontological theorists look to the underlying principles of an action in evaluating its moral worth. But despite the diversity, by far the most influential
moral theories in Western thought since Descartes have founded morality
upon reason.

A less influential alternative perspective concerning morality has per-
sisted which rejects the exclusion of emotion from the moral realm. In its
theories various emotions such as love and sympathy are seen as moral capacities. It is argued, for example, that it is our ability to recognize and
sympathetically share the reactions of others to certain actions that enables
us to properly identify moral actions. Theorists of this alternative perspective
generally do not reject reason from the moral realm, but they do not see it
as the ultimate source of morality. Reason rather becomes a guide to the
emotions, providing general rules to direct and regulate feeling.

Given my discussion of the maleness of reason and the association of

---

* It is important to remember that not all men were seen as fully masculine, only those
from groups viewed as the most civilized.

women with emotion, one would expect women to fare better with the latter theory in which moral action is viewed as having an emotional component than with the former theory in which moral action must be based on reason alone. In order to investigate this prediction, I will compare the moral theories of Immanuel Kant (1724–1804) and David Hume (1711–1776). In the philosophy of Kant, the tenet that moral action must be based solely on reason receives its fullest and most influential development. Hume's ethical theory, in contrast to Kant's, founds moral action on the sentiments and affections of humans.

My question in this chapter is similar to that discussed in the previous chapter, now applied to moral theory; that is, is morality male? Like the previous question, this question raises numerous issues. Are women viewed as incapable or less capable of being moral agents? In depicting the moral individual, do moral theorists emphasize traits traditionally associated with masculinity and men? Is the source of women's moral actions perceived to be different than that of men? That is, are women seen as possessing a different moral voice?[1] Is the attainment of moral agency viewed as involving the control or transcendence of traits historically identified as female?

THE MORALITY OF REASON: KANT

Kant's philosophy has been a major cause of the emphasis in nineteenth- and twentieth-century moral theory on a moral rationalism, that is, the view that moral principles are known solely through reason where reason is defined, following Descartes, as excluding the emotions. In the *Grounding for the Metaphysics of Morals*, Kant argues that an action must be performed from duty alone in order to have moral worth. An action resulting from inclination, even if it happens to accord with duty, is precluded from the moral realm. Giving the example of a person who is naturally sympathetic and who desires to help those in need, Kant maintains "that in such a case an action of this kind, however dutiful and amiable it may be, has nevertheless no true moral worth."[2] It is not Kant's intention to imply that a person acts morally only when her or his actions are similarly devoid of any desire or inclination toward such an action. He simply offers this as a situation in which we know with certainty that the individual acted morally, for there can be no question of the action arising partly from desire or inclination. Kant's point is that an individual's desires and inclinations, whether positive or negative, are not a part of moral action. Still, Kant views inclinations as so undesirable that he claims that "the universal wish of every rational being must be, rather, to be wholly free from them."[3] Actions done from duty must, according to Kant, completely exclude the influence of inclination. One who is moved by compassion to assist a drowning child does not act purely out of respect for the moral law and thus, on Kant's account, does not act morally. Although admitting that such actions deserve praise and encouragement, Kant denies that they deserve esteem, for they lack moral content. It is only the person whose action is totally divorced from her or his desires or inclinations who is capable of acting from duty. As an example, Kant describes a person whose mind is "clouded over with his own sorrow so that all sympathy with the lot of others is extinguished . . . he nevertheless tears himself from this deadly insensibility and performs the action without any inclination at all, but solely from duty."[4] Only then does this individual's action have moral worth.

Kantian moral persons, then, must learn to distance themselves from their emotions and desires. Even such feelings as sympathy, caring, love, honor, and altruism are at best irrelevant to the action of a moral agent, and at worst they constitute a hindrance. It is not necessary that moral persons be without affect, but they must be able to suspend their feelings in order to base their action on obedience to the universal law of morality, for "only the law itself can be an object of respect and hence can be a command."[5] For Kant, this law is the categorical imperative: "I should never act except in such a way that I can also will that my maxim should become a universal law."[6] The categorical imperative is a principle of action, a law, which is objectively necessary in itself without reference to another end. An action based on the categorical imperative is inherently good regardless of the intended or actual consequences of the action. Its goodness arises from the form of the action and the principle from which it follows.

The law of morality is objective, holding for all beings and for all times.[7] Moral principles should, according to Kant, "be derived from the universal concept of a rational being in general, since moral laws should hold for every rational being as such."[8] Morality is, for Kant, based on reason and known only through reason. First, Kant argues that only a rational being is capable of acting according to the law. Second, he believes that derivation of moral actions from the categorical imperative is based solely on reason.

Having established the universal form of the categorical imperative, Kant asks a question: "Is it a necessary law for all rational beings always to judge their actions according to such maxims as they can themselves will that such should serve as universal laws?"[9] He offers an affirmative answer by demonstrating that there is an inherent connection between the law and the will of a rational being. Returning again to the example of the person who assists individuals who are in need not because she or he is so inclined, but rather because it is her or his duty to do so, Kant argues that such an action has an end. According to Kant, the unconditionally valuable end of the categorical imperative is the "right of humanity." "Although the conformity of actions to right (i.e., being an upright man) is nothing meritorious, yet the conformity to right of the maxim of such actions regarded as duties, i.e., *respect* for right, is meritorious. For by this latter conformity a man makes the right of humanity or of men his end."[10]

The characteristic that makes the right of humanity the unconditional end of all moral action is humanity's rationality.

The capacity to propose an end to oneself is the characteristic of humanity (as distinguished from animality). The rational will is therefore bound up with the end of the humanity in our own person, as is also, consequently, the duty to deserve well of humanity by means of culture in general, and to acquire or promote the capacity of carrying out all sorts of ends, as far as this capacity is to be found in man.[11]

That which gives humans inherent value and which sets them apart from other animals is their capacity to act from reason rather than instinct, choosing the maxims of their actions. It is because of this capacity that it would be wrong under any circumstance to treat another, or one's self, as a means. Thus, Kant concludes that every rational being "exists as an end in himself and not merely as a means to be arbitrarily used by this or that will."[12] Kant derives what he calls the practical imperative from his conclusion that all rational beings possess inherent value: "Act in such a way that you treat humanity, whether in your own person or in the person of another, always at the same time as an end and never simply as a means."[13] The categorical imperative is the form of the moral law, while the rational nature of humans is the material of the law.

Since humanity is the end of moral action, and what makes humanity an end is rational choice, only when choice is fully rational is humanity fully realized. Thus to do anything to limit or hinder rational choice, your own or that of another, regardless of the reason, diminishes the good.[14] According to Kant our obligations are twofold: a negative obligation to never act in such a manner as to impede any person's rational capacities and a positive obligation to act to bring about full realization of our own rational capacities.

As an example of the first obligation, Kant considers the duty not to commit suicide. Kant argues that "to dispose of oneself as a mere means to some end of one's own liking is to degrade the humanity in one's person (*homo noumenon*), which, after all, was entrusted to man (*homo phaenomenon*) to preserve."[15] Such an action would be, on Kant's analysis, contradictory. To destroy oneself is to obliterate the very existence of morality. Suicide cannot constitute an end, for it is the individual as a rational being who makes an action an end and thus confers value upon it. But, self-destruction would result in the absence of ends, and thus suicide by its very nature cannot be made an end for this action destroys the individual who would confer value upon it. Hence, suicide can never be a rational act.

An example of the second obligation is the duty to perfect oneself. Kant charges individuals to "cultivate your powers of mind and body so as to be able to fulfill all the ends which may arise for you."[16] In other words, individuals are to develop the physical and mental capacities that will enable them to fully employ their powers of rational choice. Kant, like Descartes, believing that we can cultivate our rational capacities, holds that the full development of our rational capacities, self-perfection, is a duty.

Self-perfection involves cultivating autonomy, a trait Kant perceives as a fundamental feature of moral persons. "Autonomy is the ground of the dignity of human nature and of every rational nature."[17] To be autonomous, one must act independently of any influence, whether that influence be internal, that is, based on one's inclinations, or external, based on the will of another. Thus, an individual is capable of moral action only if her or his actions are subject to no influence, that is, only if she or he freely chooses the good. "An absolutely good will, whose principle must be a categorical imperative, will therefore be indeterminate as regards all objects and will contain merely the form of willing; and indeed that form is autonomy. This is to say that the fitness of the maxims of every good will to make themselves universal laws is itself the only law that the will of every rational being imposes on itself, without needing to assume any incentive or interest as a basis."[18]

The importance of autonomy in Kant's philosophy applies to the political as well as the moral realm. Kant argues that the state will be just only if those framing and voting on the laws governing it create political conditions which place humanity as an end. Thus, citizens, like the morally just individual, must act solely on the basis of reason. However, citizens can act rationally only to the extent that they are subject to no influence other than their rational will. Thus Kant concludes that those with full citizenship, or what he labels "active citizens," must have an "independent position among the people." In contrast, what he calls passive citizens, those who "depend for their living (i.e. for food and protection) on the offices of others (excluding the state)— all of these people have no civil personality."[19] Only fully autonomous persons are capable of making the good the sole principle of their actions.

Having clarified Kant's moral theory, I will now turn to Kant's views concerning woman. An obvious place to begin this examination of the Kantian view of woman's nature is with his discussion of the two sexes in his *Observations on the Feeling of the Beautiful and Sublime.* Kant, like Rousseau, subscribed to the view that the sexes possess complementary natures. He refers to woman as the fair or beautiful sex, and to man as the noble sex. Like Rousseau, Kant does not hold that women totally lack noble qualities, or that men possess nothing of the beautiful. He holds rather that "a person of either sex brings both together, in such a way that all the other merits of a woman should unite solely to enhance the character of the beautiful, which is the proper reference point; and on the other hand among the masculine qualities the sublime clearly stands out as the criterion of his kind."[20] Kant insists that any attempt to encourage moral perfection or to praise or blame an individual must refer to these criteria.

Kant attributes to women "a strong inborn feeling for all that is beautiful, elegant, and decorated."[21] In a passage which clearly illustrates Rousseau's influence, Kant explains that girls as well as women love adornment and are delicate, modest, and self-possessed. Accepting the traditional association of woman with emotionality, Kant asserts that women "have many sympathetic sensations, goodheartedness, and compassion."[22] Like Rousseau, Kant believes that such qualities enable women to refine men.

It is important to note that Kant is not here describing all women, but is rather offering his views concerning the female of the European bourgeoisie. This strong, inborn feeling for the beautiful will be absent in those women Kant labels as "uncivilized." In fact, Kant's view of the complementarity of the sexes does not apply universally. While civilized women and men evince complementary areas of superiority, Kant views the uncivilized woman as in no way man's superior. "As *culture* advances, each party must be superior in his own particular way: the man must be superior to the woman by his physical strength and courage; the woman to the man, however, by her natural talent for gaining mastery over his desire for her. In a still uncivilized state, on the contrary, all superiority is on the man's side."[23] Although civilization does not cause woman's "charm," Kant believes that it does enable such feminine characteristics to develop. Thus, the Kantian view of different but equal can at best hold only for "civilized" women.

Kant's view that women are more emotional than men need not necessarily imply that their moral capacity would be inferior to or different from that of man. As I explained earlier, Kant does not require that moral individuals be devoid of all feeling or inclination; they simply must not base their actions upon it. In fact Kant recognizes moral feelings such as conscience, love of one's neighbor, and respect for one's self; Kant argues that "no man is devoid of all moral feeling; for if he were totally unsusceptible to this sensation, he would be morally dead."[24] But while such moral feelings offer an initial understanding of the good, Kant insists that even feelings such as these must not be a basis of action if one is to act morally.

Kant, however, additionally holds that women are less rational than men, and this, unlike his belief that women are more emotional, does entail that woman's moral capacity is not the same as man's. Arguing that the "civilized" woman has as much understanding as the "civilized" man, Kant argues that the woman's understanding is different from that of the man. Hers is a "beautiful understanding," while his is a "noble understanding." While women easily and immediately perceive the beauty of an action, Kant excludes them from "deep meditation and a long-sustained reflection."[25] In other words,

"Women will avoid the wicked not because it is unright, but because it is ugly; and virtuous actions mean to them such as are morally beautiful. Nothing of duty, nothing of compulsion, nothing of obligation!"[26] Kant is here referring only to "civilized" women. The "uncivilized" woman, being less able to recognize the beautiful, is less capable of avoiding the wicked. In developing his moral theory, Kant saw himself as describing only the natures of women and men from what he called "civilized" and "cultivated" races, listing England and France as the two most civilized nations on earth.[27] Women and men from non-European nations were not seen by Kant as being sufficiently developed to fully possess either a beautiful or a noble understanding. He asserts, for example, that "the Negroes of Africa have by nature no feeling that rises above the trifling . . . so fundamental is the difference between these two races of man [blacks and whites], and it appears to be as great in regard to mental capacities as in color."[28]

Turning now to Kant's views of the moral nature of "civilized" women and men, we see that Kant, like Rousseau, viewed the source of woman's morality as different from that of man. The moral man uses reason to determine what is right and acts on the basis of duty. Woman does not act on principle, but rather bases her actions on inclination. Even her moral instruction is to be different from that of man. "One will seek to broaden their [women's] total moral feeling and not their memory, and that of course not by universal rules but by some judgment upon the conduct that they see about them."[29] Woman's moral instruction is not to be cold and speculative, but rather based on feelings.

A clear tension arises at this point. Since Kant defines moral action as action based on reason in accord with the categorical imperative but perceives woman as incapable of such principles, it appears we must conclude that woman cannot act morally.* Kant attempts to avoid this rather undesirable conclusion by insisting that woman is virtuous, but that hers is a beautiful rather than noble virtue. Unfortunately, this device is not adequate, for it constitutes a mere case of relabeling on Kant's part. In an earlier passage, Kant distinguishes between "adoptive virtues," those actions which are in accordance with moral law but are based on moral feelings such as kindheartedness rather than reason, and "genuine virtue," action which rests upon principles. The former virtues, although admirable, are for Kant not true virtues. But what Kant labels "beautiful virtues" in woman are simply "adoptive virtues." We are left with the conclusion that although a woman can be

* In the remainder of my discussion of Kant, I will use the terms "woman" and "women" to refer only to the group of women classified by Kant as civilized. Kant's racism—his belief in the inferiority of the non-European races of peoples—is silently inscribed throughout his discussion of women and morality, for the virtues he attributes to women apply only to those he classifies as civilized.

good, she is not moral. On Kant's theory even the best and most "cultivated" of women, those women whose actions are always in accord with duty, will not be acting morally because their actions will be based on moral feeling. Thus, the good woman is amoral.

It appears that Kant's universal principle of human conduct is far from universal. But this is inconsistent with Kant's view that the categorical imperative is derived from the universal concept of a rational being. Kant cannot claim in one breath that his moral theory applies to all rational beings and in the next breath deny that women are capable of moral action, unless, of course, he was willing to deny that women are rational beings.

At first glance, there do seem to be passages one might view as entailing the position that Kant did not perceive woman as capable of reason. Kant tells us that woman's "philosophy is not to reason, but to sense."[30] In his *Anthropology*, he argues that nature "designed" woman for two purposes: (1) to preserve the species, and (2) to improve and refine society. Because women bear the embryo, nature "implanted fear into the woman's character." In other words, Kant sees woman as less capable than man of developing courage because of her role in procreation. Similarly, woman has by nature "modesty and eloquence in speech and expression."[31] We could correctly conclude that Kant held that there are biological differences between the sexes, but it would be wrong to infer that one of these differences is that woman lack the rational faculty. On the contrary, Kant explicitly states that woman is a rational being. "It [nature] provided the man with greater strength than the woman in order to bring them together into the most intimate *physical* union, which, insofar as they are still *rational* beings too, it orders to the end most important to it, the preservation of the species."[32] We thus cannot but conclude that Kant believes that women do possess the capacity to develop moral character. So why does he hold that women will base their actions on inclination rather than reason?

If we look carefully at Kant's discussion of woman's rational capacity, we find that he did not deny that women were capable of rational analysis and thus incapable of action based on principle. Rather, he thought it *unwise* for women to develop this capacity. For example, Kant does not say that deep meditation and long-sustained reflection are impossible for women, but rather that they "do not well befit" her. Such activities, "even if a woman should greatly succeed in [them], destroy the merits that are proper to her sex . . . at the same time they will weaken the charms with which she exercises her great power over the other sex."[33]

What are these charms that a developed rational faculty would weaken? They are those traits Kant sees as needed for woman to perform her two innate functions successfully: procreation and refinement of society. Among them Kant includes a feeling for the beautiful, a modest manner, a love of pleasantry, sympathy and good-heartedness, a sensitivity to the "finer" feelings, propriety, and a complaisant soul.[34] Kant believes that women's virtues, and thus also their vices, are very different from those of men.

She should be *patient*; he must be *tolerant*. She is *sensitive*; he is *responsive.*—Man's economic system consists in *acquiring*, woman's in *saving.*—The man is jealous *when he loves*; the woman is jealous even when she does not love, because every admirer gained by other women is one lost to her circle of suitors.—The man has taste while *on his own*: the woman makes herself the object of *everyone's* taste.[35]

Woman's beautiful understanding is to be directed not to science or history or philosophy, but to "humankind, and among humanity, men."[36] It is Kant's belief that women's differences are well suited to encouraging men to develop their perfections, both intellectual and moral. Women, Kant tells us, are attracted by noble qualities in men, that is, by wisdom, courage, and accomplishments. Men, in turn attracted by women's beauty, are thereby stimulated to develop their noble characteristics.

Kant thus believes that women's differences, although desirable, are not inevitable. The only sex differences that Kant viewed as biological are timidity and modesty. Yet his list of differences between the sexes goes far beyond these two. We must inquire, therefore, into the source of the remaining differences. Kant clearly believes that women are capable of intellectual accomplishments, citing Mme. Dacier and the Marquise de Chatelet as examples. Yet Kant argues that the education of women should not be directed to the development of their rational capacities. Women's education is rather to be designed to assist them in fitting properly into what Kant perceived to be their appropriate social roles: wives and mothers. "A woman's education is not instruction, but guidance. She must know men rather than books. Honor is her greatest virtue, domesticity her merit."[37] Thus it appears that at least a portion of the differences in the rational capacities of the sexes is due to women's socialization.*

Thus the inconsistency in Kant's theory that I noted earlier reappears. Kant views the development of the rational capacities as necessary for the

---

* I believe that an argument can be made that removing the effects of socialization upon woman's rational capacities would not completely remove the sex differences subscribed to by Kant. In his essay "What is Enlightenment?" Kant claims that courage is needed for rational action. Since Kant clearly views woman as innately timid due to her procreative role, it follows that he would have denied that she would be as courageous as man. Hence, if he associates courage and rational ability, he will not hold that women are as capable of rationality as men. However, it does not follow from this that women are incapable of rational thought, nor does this justify in any way hindering the development of their rational capacities. At best, Kant might conclude that women are less likely than man to achieve moral agency, but not that they are incapable.

formation of a moral character, yet argues against the education of women's rational abilities. He gives as his reason that such an education would "weaken the charms with which she exercises her great power over the other sex."[38] In other words, woman's rational capacities are not to be inculcated because doing so would inhibit *man's* development. But that implies that woman is being treated as a *means* rather than an end. Setting up an impediment to the advancement of her rational abilities is not good in itself, but is good because it enables her to serve as an inspiration to man. But treating any rational being as a means to an end is completely at odds with Kant's practical imperative: act in such a way that you treat humanity always as an end and never simply as a means.

If we look carefully at Kant's discussion of woman's nature, we discover that all the qualities that make woman beautiful—her charm, her inborn feeling for the beautiful, her good-heartedness and other gentle qualities— acquire a large portion if not all of their value from their benefit to man. Kant does not claim that these feminine characteristics are inherently valuable, but rather discusses the ways in which they ennoble man. The good woman takes advantage of "the impression that the form and features of the fair sex make on the masculine," which Kant sees as overlaid upon the sex instinct, to bind a man to his children and encourage him to perfect his character.[39] Kant apparently believes that nature itself sets up man as the end of humanity and woman as the means of his perfection. "The purposes of nature are directed still more to ennoble man, by the sexual inclination, and likewise still more to beautify woman. A woman is embarrassed little that she does not possess certain high insights, that she is timid, and not fit for serious employments, and so forth; she is beautiful and captivates, and that is enough."[40]

Kant believes that this does not imply that woman is man's inferior, but rather that each is in a different way the superior of the other. Woman, Kant tells us, is man's superior in respect to "her natural talent for gaining mastery over his desire for her."[41] But woman's superiority is in the area of the senses, not reason, of inclination, not duty. Her superiority is thus a double-edged sword. It has the potential of instilling the more refined feelings, but since it is a power of the senses over reason and of inclination over duty, unless it is carefully contained and controlled by man, it will lead neither to knowledge nor to morality.[42]

As I noted earlier in explicating the practical imperative, Kant argues that people have a duty to perfect themselves. "It is the duty of man to himself to cultivate his natural powers (of the spirit, of the mind, and of the body)."[43] Yet Kant is arguing against this cultivation by woman, not because she is biologically incapable of developing these powers, but because it would make her less effective in her social role. Kant's views on the education of women, then, are in direct tension with his own practical imperative, and are thus immoral.

It appears that the tension in the Kantian philosophy concerning woman rests not upon Kant's views concerning woman's rational abilities, but rather upon his beliefs concerning woman's role. His claim that woman's function is to improve and refine society sets up an unresolvable tension. A feature of being rational is an individual's ability to choose her or his own purposes, that is, to act based on rational choice, free from the influence of inclinations as well as any external influences.[44] But Kant admits that woman's role precludes this ability. The conclusion that would have been consistent with Kant's moral theory is *not* that women's education should be carefully geared to fitting women to their roles as wives and mothers so that they can refine man, but rather that women's education should be changed and every effort made to assist them in fully developing their own rational capacities, thus enabling women to become capable of moral agency. It appears that with Kant we have an illustration of the claim I made in Chapter Three when examining the philosophy of Descartes that a theory of rationality, or in this case a moral theory, that rests upon a conception of rationality that defines rationality as masculine, will result in the belief that a woman can follow the "life of the mind" only to the extent that she renounces all activities and characteristics that define her as feminine. Not only will the attainment of the rational life be seen as more difficult for a woman, it will not be uncommon to find those, like Kant and Rousseau, who argue that the attempt to attain it on the part of women would undermine the fabric of society.

Since the contradiction here is so obvious, why did Kant not see it?* I believe this question can be answered by investigating Kant's views concerning the marriage relationship.[45] "In matrimonial life," Kant tells us, "the united pair should, as it were, constitute a single moral person, which is animated and governed by the understanding of the man and the taste of the wife." Man possesses "more insight founded on experience," while woman has "more freedom and accuracy in sensation."[46] What we discover is that Kant subscribes to Rousseau's view of the complementarity of the sexes. Man contributes reason and insight, woman contributes emotions and empathy. The problem is that Kant combines this Rousseauean view of the nature of

* Although lack of space precludes discussion of the historical context of Kant's beliefs, I do not mean to slight the fact that Kant himself was influenced by the social and cultural milieu in which he lived. His beliefs were, of course, influenced by the mores of eighteenth-century Prussia and the particularities of his own upbringing. It has recently been argued, for example, that Kant was strongly influenced by his pietistic background. Nevertheless, the tension I noted above is one which touches the very heart of his moral theory. It is a tension so obvious that Kant should have been aware of it. My point, then, is that the force of prejudice was so powerful that it blinded Kant to the very implications of his own theory.

the marriage relationship with a Cartesian view of reason. While supporting the importance of a woman's finer sensibilities for her role as a mother and inspiration to her husband, Kant views reason alone as the source of knowledge and morality.

Kant allows that women can be good; they can be good wives and mothers. But they are not capable of moral goodness. "The principal object [of marriage] is that the man should become more perfect as a man, and the woman as a wife."[47] Only man's goodness is absolute. Even when Kant praises a woman's goodness, he is praising her goodness as a wife rather than as a good person. In his example of Milton's wife, Kant tells us that she encouraged her husband to take a political position despite the fact that doing so would be contrary to his principles. Milton, refuses her request. " 'Ah, my dear,' he replied; 'you and the rest of your sex want to travel in coaches: but I— must be an honorable man.' " Kant tells us that she is an exemplar of women who "within their own households, maintained creditably a character in keeping with their vocation."[48] In other words, she was a good wife, but one who could only perceive the practical worth rather than the moral worth of an action.

Despite his view of the complementarity of civilized women and men, Kant did not hold that they should be equals. The position of woman in marriage is not one of equality, but of dependence. "A *woman*, regardless of her age, is under civil tutelage [or incompetent to speak for herself (*unmundig*)]; her husband is her natural curator.[49] Kant bases this "curatorship" upon woman's natural weakness, that is, the fear and timidity originating from woman's role in procreation, and argues that the protection of man is a right of woman, not a liability. Despite Kant's protests, this "right" *is* a liability, for it makes woman dependent upon man.

Kant offers an additional reason for woman's dependence upon man. "If a union is to be harmonious and indissoluble . . . one party must be *subject* to the other and, reciprocally, one must be the *superior* of the other in some way, in order to be able to rule and govern him."[50] Although Kant argued that in a state of peace, government would consist of cooperation among men, he rejected this possibility within the marriage relationship. "If two people who cannot dispense with each other make equal *claims*, self-love produces nothing but wrangling. As *culture* advances, each party must be superior in his own particular way."[51]

Kant attempts to soften his position by explaining that although the husband will "govern," the wife will "reign." "Who, then, should have supreme command in the household?—for there can be only one person who co-ordinates all occupations in accordance with one end, which is his.—I would say, in the language of gallantry (but not without truth): the woman should *reign* and the man *govern*; for inclination reigns and understanding governs."[52] Upon examination, reigning turns out to be a very hollow role. Kant likened the reign of the wife to that of a "monarch who thinks only of amusement." The husband, according to Kant, should be compliant with his wife's desires, but since only he is capable of judging which actions are best, *he must tell her what her will consists of!* "The monarch can do all that he wills, but on one condition: that his minister lets him know what his will is."[53]

This dependence upon their husbands' will excludes women from the political as well as the moral realm. Kant views autonomy as a precondition for moral action yet rejects the possibility of woman's autonomy. A woman, Kant tells us, does not choose the maxim of her action. Her actions are determined through inclination and the will of her husband. Her lack of autonomy additionally excludes her from full citizenship. A woman will be a passive citizen with no right "to guide the state, to organize, and to work for introduction of particular laws."[54] Woman is thus not man's equal in the state. All men are capable of attaining active citizenship. But women, because of their relation to men, are not and cannot become active citizens.

This too reveals an inconsistency in Kant's philosophy. Kant claims that the civil laws and institutions must be compatible "with the natural laws of freedom and with the equality that accords with this freedom, namely, that everyone be able to work up from this passive state to an active status."[55] Since women are incapable of attaining the status of active citizenship, they are, by this definition, denied full rights of equality. Kant's view that freedom and equality are natural laws, laws that should not be overturned by civic conventions, entails that if a woman's social role precludes her achieving freedom and independence, then her role should be altered. In other words, Kant's position concerning freedom dictates that women's education be altered to encourage development of their rational faculties and that marriage relationships be based on cooperation rather than subjugation—just the opposite of Kant's stance on these issues.

This investigation of the maleness of morality in the Kantian scheme thus reveals a number of inconsistencies in Kant's philosophy. While arguing for the universality of his moral principles, we find that they do not in fact apply to women. Women, although potentially capable of moral agency, are, according to Kant, to be educated in such a way that they will be unable to actually achieve it. Women are thus incapable of moral agency, not because of a biological deficiency of the kind Aristotle would have argued for, but rather because their social role precludes full development of their rational faculties. A woman is thus limited to actions based on inclination. She is at best worthy of praise, never of esteem.

As with Descartes' notion of reason, the traits that Kant associates with the moral person—rational action, autonomy, detachment, acting from universal principles, controlling inclinations, adherence to duty and obligation

—are characteristics that Kant, in keeping with his culture, associated with masculinity. Some traits considered feminine, like dependency, are seen by Kant as precluding moral agency. Others, like sympathy and compassion, at best simply assist one in acting appropriately; they are never those characteristics associated with moral agency.[56] Kantian morality is thus male and the Kantian moral person is a man, albeit a "civilized" one.

THE MORALITY OF EMOTIONS: HUME

Kant was strongly influenced by the philosophy of David Hume, claiming that it was Hume who had awakened him from his "dogmatic slumber." Nevertheless, Kant and Hume hold radically different views concerning the role of reason in morality. While Kant believed that in order for an action to be fully moral, it must not be based on the passions, Hume took the opposite position that moral actions arise out of the passions. Thus in Hume we find a potential theory of morality that includes, and perhaps even privileges, those traits which have traditionally been perceived as feminine. I will begin by describing Hume's views on morality with an emphasis upon highlighting the role of the feminine within his moral philosophy. Having delineated the ways in which the Kantian moral person is male, I will here question whether the Humean moral person is similarly gendered. Or is Hume's moral theory one in which the moral person is just that—a person?

Hume begins his *Enquiry Concerning the Principles of Morals* with a discussion of the controversy as to whether the foundation of morals is reason or sentiment. Advancing arguments for both sides, Hume concludes "that *reason* and *sentiment* concur in almost all moral determinations and conclusions."[57] Thus Hume, unlike Kant, includes the passions within the moral realm, though he also acknowledges the role of reason.

Hume contends that moral action would be impossible if humans did not possess an innate moral sense or feeling. However, reason is also needed in order to properly discern the object of our sentiment. Having determined that the usefulness of a quality or action is the basis of its moral worth,* Hume explains that it is reason that must show us this utility.[58] "*Reason* must enter for a considerable share in all decisions of this kind; since nothing but that faculty can instruct us in the tendency of qualities and actions, and point out their beneficial consequences to society and to their possessor."[59] Hume thus does not derogate the function of reason within the moral realm; but he also does not limit the moral to the rational.

---

* Hume is quite vague about this notion of utility, but he clearly depicts a uniformity or "near uniformity" of judgment concerning an action's utility. Although I will not pursue it, there appears to be reason to believe that this tenet carries a gender, as well as a race and class, bias.

Hume explains that although reason can instruct us in the utility of an action or a quality and can reveal to us the best means to achieve it, it cannot cause us to prefer that action or quality, nor to act in order to achieve it. That is, should we remain indifferent to that which is useful, we will not act in such a way as to bring it about. Thus, Hume concludes that

it is requisite a *sentiment* should here display itself, in order to give a preference to the useful above the pernicious tendencies. This sentiment can be no other than a feeling for the happiness of mankind, and a resentment of their misery; since these are the different ends which virtue and vice have a tendency to promote. Here therefore *reason* instructs us in the several tendencies of actions, and *humanity* makes a distinction in favour of those which are useful and beneficial.[60]

Hume, taking a very different stance from that adopted by Kant, argues that the dispassionate nature of reason would preclude its functioning as a motive to action. Only the sentiment of beauty or usefulness can serve as a stimulus for action. We act to assist the drowning child because we are moved by the suffering of the child and by the suffering of the child's family should she or he drown, and we know that saving the child is in the interest of all involved: the child, her or his family, and ourself. The motive for saving the drowning child is very different for the Humean moral person than the motive might be for the Kantian moral individual.

The moral person, for Hume, is the individual of feeling. The sentiment Hume emphasizes over all others is benevolence. "Nothing can bestow more merit on any human creature than the sentiment of benevolence in an eminent degree; and *that* a *part*, at least, of its merit arises from its tendency to promote the interests of our species, and bestow happiness on human society."[61] The list of characteristics that describe a moral person include sociability, good-naturedness, humaneness, mercy, gratefulness, friendliness, generosity, beneficence, tenderness, sympathy, fairness, and greatness of mind.[62]

All individuals, Hume tells us, have some degree of innate benevolence. He insists that we cannot without great absurdity deny that "there is some benevolence, however small, infused into our bosom; some spark of friendship for human kind; some particle of the dove kneaded into our frame, along with the elements of the wolf and serpent."[63] Without such sentiments, Hume explains, one would never be moved to act. And benevolence is tied to sympathy, for it is through sympathy that an individual responds to the needs of another. "When I see the *effects* of passion in the voice and gesture of any person, my mind immediately passes from these effects to their causes, and forms such a lively idea of the passion, as is presently converted into the passion itself."[64] Through sympathy we experience the feelings of another. Because of this connection with another's feelings we come to desire her or his happiness. Thus it is because of our empathy with the suffering of the drowning child and the grief of the child's family that we desire that the child be rescued.

Hume concludes that the moral individual acts to bring about happiness and satisfaction. Interestingly, he begins his description of the moral person by focusing upon the private realm. He tells us that moral persons are characterized by their "pious attachment" to and "duteous care" of their parents, the loving guidance they offer their children, and the support and consideration they give to their domestics. In addition, moral individuals are good and loving friends who possess the virtue of being able to gain and keep the trust of others. Furthermore they are always ready to help those in need. Never one for understatement, Hume characterizes the moral individual thus: "Like the sun, an inferior minister of providence he cheers, invigorates, and sustains the surrounding world."[65]

But the moral individual must also have recourse to reason in order to adjudicate between conflicting needs and to follow the rules of morality. Hume does not deny that there are rules of justice which the moral individual must follow, but he does not see these rules, as will Kant, as universal, that is, valid for all people at all times and places. According to Hume, these rules are contingent, determined by various conditions and customs of different communities and different periods. "The rules of equity or justice depend entirely on the particular state and condition in which men are placed, and owe their origin and existence to that utility, which results to the public from their strict and regular observance."[66] The role of reason, then, in "the correction of sentiment" is to guide the actions of the moral individual, clarifying the consequences of different courses of actions and mediating conflicts between the needs of different individuals. The moral individual must therefore act from both head and heart.[67]

Hume's writings thus offer a moral theory which emphasizes traits stereotypically associated with the feminine: the passions and a concern with the relations between people. Looking again at the list of characteristics that Hume uses to describe the moral individual—sociability, good-naturedness, humaneness, mercy, gratefulness, friendliness, generosity, beneficence, tenderness, sympathy, fairness, and greatness of mind—reveals that many of them are traits associated with women in Europe in the eighteenth century.* It is

---

* In the eighteenth century a new biology was embraced which deviated from the Aristotelian notion of woman as a misbegotten man—what Thomas Laqueur called a biology based on the "metaphysics of hierarchy" ("Orgasm, Generation, and the Politics of Reproductive Biology," in *The Making of the Modern Body*, eds. Catherine Gallagher and Thomas Laqueur (Berkeley: University of California Press, 1987, p 3). The new biology advocated a theory of complementarity between the sexes. Woman, then, was not seen as an inferior man, but rather as perfect in her own right. However, her "own right" continued to parallel earlier conceptions. Eighteenth-century biologists, much like Aristotle, depicted women as, by nature, passive, dependent, modest, domestic, and maternal.

women who have been seen as the sex most moved by the passions to sympathize with those in need, women who have been characterized as tender, as sociable, as grateful, as friendly. Hume's concern with the private realm of familial relations, a realm traditionally assigned to women, is an indication that Hume's moral theory, unlike Kant's, is not male.[68]

Furthermore, although retaining a division between reason and emotion, Hume reverses the Cartesian privileging of reason over emotion. "Reason is, and ought only to be the slave of the passions, and can never pretend to any other office than to serve and obey them."[69] The Humean moral person is the opposite of the Kantian dispassionate, disinterested, autonomous individual. Given his emphasis on emotion over reason, his attention to the moral importance of relationships between people, and the types of traits ascribed to the moral individual, I believe it fair to conclude that Humean moral theory is feminine, or perhaps more fairly that it is androgynous, with an emphasis on the feminine.[70] In this sense, Hume's moral theory can be seen as more balanced than that of Kant. Whereas Kant excludes emotions from the moral realm, Hume recognizes the importance of a balance of reason and emotion. Whereas the characteristics of a Kantian moral individual are male, the Humean moral person blends female and male traits: is sympathetic but fair, passionate yet reasonable.

It would, however, be premature to conclude from this that the Humean moral person is not "gendered," that is, that Hume perceived women as just as capable of moral goodness as men. As we have seen, women have often been seen as incapable or as less capable than men of reason. Therefore, since Hume's moral individual must be capable of *reason* as well as emotion, it is not obvious that women will be viewed as possessing an identical capacity for moral development. However, the reverse is not the case for men. Men have not been viewed as incapable of emotion. Emotion, often perceived as an inferior faculty of the mind, has been traditionally credited to women and men alike. But reason, seen as a more developed faculty of the mind, has been attributed only to those individuals seen as most evolved or "civilized"—typically upper-class, European males. Thus the question remains, Is the Humean moral person "gendered"?

If we look at Hume's discussion of the moral person, it is clear that he was envisioning a man. He tells us, for example, that "when we enumerate the good qualities of any person, we always mention those parts of his character, which render him a safe companion, an easy friend, a gentle master, an agreeable husband, or an indulgent father."[71] Similarly, at the end of the *Enquiry*, Hume presents us with a man, Cleanthes, as his model of the moral individual. It is thus important to determine if his description of the moral individual as male is simply a symptom of the sex bias of Hume's culture which he unwittingly inscribed on his moral theory, or if there is an aspect of his moral theory which necessitates the exclusion of women from the moral realm. It is to this question I now turn.

Let us look more closely at Cleanthes, the "model of perfect virtue." We are told that Cleanthes is a man of honor and humanity who treats everyone fairly and with kindness. He is dedicated to his profession, which, in combination with his insight into the nature of people, promises "the greatest honours and advancement." He is sociable, witty, well-mannered, gallant, knowledgeable, and cheerful. He "preserves a perpetual serenity on his countenance, and tranquillity in his soul," for despite trials, misfortunes, and dangers, "his greatness of mind, was still superior to all of them."[72]

Hume makes the image of Cleanthes clearer by offering a list of vices he does not have: "celibacy, fasting, penance, mortification, self-denial, humility, silence, solitude, and the whole train of monkish virtues."[73] These, Hume claims, serve no purpose, and in fact hinder an individual by stupefying the understanding and hardening the heart.

The question before us is whether there is anything in Hume's moral theory which precludes a female Cleanthes. Hume remains relatively silent concerning the subject of women. However, he offers a discourse on the virtue of chastity in women and also offers scattered remarks concerning woman's nature.* I will turn to these passages in an attempt to determine whether the Humean moral person is as likely to be a woman as a man.

In his essay "On the Rise and Progress of the Arts and Sciences," Hume offers an aside on the topic of gallantry. Having discussed the Roman custom of honoring first the person of the greatest distinction, Hume refers to the modern notion of offering respect and deference to one's inferiors, what he calls "gallantry." Arguing against the Roman custom, Hume argues that modern gallantry is both generous and natural, in that it keeps us from causing injury to others and renders intercourse between people more agreeable. "A polite man," Hume tells us, "learns to behave with deference towards his companions, and to yield the superiority to them in all the common incidents of society."[74] Hume then turns to the relations of the sexes, arguing that in this arena, gallantry is crucial. "As nature has given *man* the superiority above *woman*, by endowing him with greater strength both of mind and body, it is his part to alleviate that superiority, as much as possible, by the generosity of his behaviour, and by a studied deference and complaisance for all her inclinations and opinions."[75] He argues that such gallantry is wise as well as generous, for without it women would be little other than the slaves of their husbands. "Barbarous nations display this superiority [i.e., of man over woman], by reducing their females to the most abject slavery."[76] Hume ex-

---

* As with Kant, the vast majority of Hume's remarks on woman's nature refer to "civilized" women, in other words, women of the European upper classes.

plains that such conditions preclude all possibility of discourse, sympathy, friendship, and gaiety between the sexes. The natural affection between the sexes thus requires the gallantry of men in order to achieve its fullest satisfaction.*

In another essay, "On the Immortality of the Soul," Hume repeats his contention that woman's mental capacities are inferior to those of men. "The inferiority of women's capacity is easily accounted for. Their domestic life requires no higher faculties either of mind or body."[77] Although this statement leaves one wondering whether Hume viewed women's intellectual and bodily inferiority as inherent or acquired, in others, such as the one cited above, there is no such ambiguity, in that Hume believes the difference to arise from nature. It appears that Hume subscribed to a position similar to that of Aristotle and quite in keeping with the European view of women in the eighteenth century: "civilized" woman is intellectually and physically inferior to "civilized" man, and her inferiority is innate.†

This interpretation receives further support from Hume's discussion of justice in his *Enquiry Concerning the Principles of Morals*. Hume poses the question of one's obligations "were there a species of creatures intermingled with men, which, though rational, were possessed of such inferior strength, both of body and mind, that they were incapable of all resistance, and could never, upon the highest provocation, make us feel the effects of their resentment."[78] His answer is that such creatures should be treated humanely, but that they possess no rights and our actions would not be governed by what Hume calls "the restraints of justice." He insists that this properly describes the relationship between men and nonhuman animals, but does not apply to the relationship between "civilized Europeans" and "barbarous Indians," nor between "civilized" men and "civilized" women.[79] In the case of "civilized" women, Hume explains that although the male superiority in bodily strength is sufficient to maintain their tyranny over women, "such are the insinuation, address, and charms of their fair companions, that women are commonly able to break the confederacy, and share with the other sex in all

---

* Hume offers a position somewhat similar to Rousseau in arguing that the company of virtuous women would "polish" a man's mind. "What better school for manners than the company of virtuous women, where the mutual endeavor to please must insensibly polish the mind, where the example of the female softness and modesty must communicate itself to their admirers, and where the delicacy of that sex puts every one on his guard, lest he give offence by any breach of decency." *Essays*, p. 134. "On the Rise and Progress of the Arts and Sciences," in *Essays: Moral, Political and Literary*, London: Oxford University Press, 1963.

† Because of Hume's racism it would be inaccurate to attribute to Hume the more general claim that women are inferior to men. He clearly saw some races of peoples, those he labeled "barbarous peoples," as inferior to others, Europeans in particular. Given this, Hume would deny that "civilized" women were inferior to all men, for he would not see them as inferior to "barbarous" men.

the rights and privileges of society."[80] "Civilized" women, thus, are to be treated with equal justice, not because they show men the error of being so treated through reasoned arguments, or act to show men this error with such courage and resolution that men are able to feel the effects of women's resentment, but rather because of their charms.*

I thus believe it fair to conclude that Hume, like Kant, perceived women to be innately inferior to men.[81] But how do we interpret women's "inferior strength of mind," and what is its significance concerning their moral abilities? Since Hume does not offer a developed discussion of the ways in which men's and women's mental capabilities differ, I will offer reasoned speculation, supported by remarks made by Hume at various places in his writings. I will begin by delineating the "strength of mind" of the moral person.

In *A Treatise of Human Nature*, Hume discusses a group of natural abilities—intelligence, good sense, judgment, wit, and eloquence—which he categorizes as virtues.† All of these are mental qualities, and all are, on Hume's reckoning, innate. Since these qualities are perceived as virtues by Hume, they are abilities we would expect to find well developed in the Humean moral person. In fact, Hume had earlier characterized Cleanthes as possessing both wit and knowledge and exhibiting fine judgment in treating all fairly.

In addition, as I have previously detailed, although Hume assigns a central role to emotion in moral action, he does not eliminate reason. "A very accurate *reason* or *judgement* is often requisite, to give the true determination, amidst such intricate doubts arising from obscure or opposite utilities."[82] The moral person thus must possess a well-developed rational capacity in order to be capable of morally correct action.

In regard to the emotions, Hume makes a distinction between calm and violent passions. The calm passions produce little emotion in the mind and are of two kinds: "either certain instincts originally implanted in our natures, such as benevolence and resentment, the love of life, and kindness to children; or the general appetite to good, and aversion to evil."[83] The violent emotions

---

* Hume is here discussing only "civilized" men and women, for "barbarous" men are unaffected by women's charms. "The people, in very temperate climates, are the most likely to attain all sorts of improvement, their blood not being so inflamed as to render them jealous, and yet being warm enough to make them set a due value on the charms and endowments of the fair sex." *Essays*, p. 220. Furthermore, Hume views Blacks as "naturally inferior to the Whites," particularly regarding strength of mind. "There scarcely ever was a civilized nation of that complexion, nor even any individual, eminent either in action or speculation." *Essays*, p. 213. Thus, black women are doubly inferior on Hume's account, for not only are they black, they are women.

† Hume lists these as virtues because they are either useful or agreeable to their possessor or to others, and thus fall under Hume's criteria for virtue.

include fear and jealousy. It is the calm passions, not the violent, that are at the heart of moral action. According to Hume, "What we call strength of mind, implies the prevalence of the calm passions above the violent."[84] The Humean moral person would exhibit such strength of mind.

What about the Humean woman? I believe it reasonable to suppose that Hume perceived woman's inferior strength of mind as affecting the degree to which she possessed the very qualities needed for moral action: a prevalence of the calm passions over the violent and an accurate judgment. Despite the fact that Hume wrote remarkably little about woman's nature, comments that support this conclusion can be found in Hume's writings.

The most telling piece of evidence is Hume's claim that "the fair sex have a great share of the tender and amorous disposition."[85] According to Hume, the amorous passion is not a calm passion, but one of "force and violence."[86] Having defined the virtuous mind as one which "reduces the affections to a just moderation," Hume offers a number of warnings about the passions of love. Hume admonishes us to base our marriages on friendship rather than love, for "love is a restless and impatient passion, full of caprices and variations arising in a moment from a feature, from an air, from nothing, and suddenly extinguishing after the same manner."[87] Furthermore, he tells us that the amorous passions, although agreeable, can "weaken and enfeeble" the mind.[88] Thus one of the weaknesses of woman's mind, her susceptibility to the passions of love, an inferiority Hume perceives as innate, inhibits her ability to properly judge the utility of actions, and thus to act virtuously.

Hume also characterizes woman as naturally timid and weak. At the end of his discussion of the reign of Queen Elizabeth in his *History of England*, a work for which he was famous in his time, Hume praises her character but admits that "we are also apt to require some more softness of disposition, some greater lenity of temper, some of those amiable weaknesses by which her sex is distinguished."[89] Describing the life of Joan of Arc, Hume lists bashfulness and timidity as traits natural to women.[90] Hume does admit that Joan was able to overcome these traits, just as Elizabeth evinced none of the amiable weakness of her sex, but it appears that it is only the extraordinary woman who is able to do so. Hume associates this weakness and timidity with women's obsession with superstition. "What age or period of life is the most addicted to superstition? The weakest and most timid. What sex? The same answer must be given. *The leaders and examples of every kind of superstition, says Strabo, are the women.*"[91] Seeing superstition as contrary to intelligence and accurate judgment, two central characteristics of the Humean moral person, we have further reason to conclude that Hume saw woman as less capable of achieving the epitome of moral development portrayed by Cleanthes.

We can find in Hume's discussion of chastity an additional reason for this conclusion concerning woman's moral capacities. The virtue of chastity is different for Hume than those of intelligence and accurate judgment, for he sees the latter as natural virtues, whereas he labels chastity an artificial virtue. Hume characterizes the natural virtues as innate propensities or dispositions that are also naturally approved of. The artificial virtues are different in that they are developed or invented, and are approved of because of social conventions. According to Hume, the artificial virtues are invented in response to the particular contexts and situations of society and are designed to enable all members of society to achieve the satisfaction of remote pleasures. Hume stresses that although they are artificial, these virtues are not arbitrary.

I have argued that Hume did not believe that the natural virtues were equally distributed between the sexes, women being less accomplished in the virtues of intelligence and accurate judgment.[92] He holds a similar position concerning the artificial virtue of chastity, arguing for a stricter rule of chastity for women. I will first examine Hume's position concerning chastity and then turn to the effects of this position on woman's ability to become the Humean moral person.

Hume devotes a chapter of his *Treatise* to arguing for the importance of the virtues of chastity and modesty in women. Although men are not fully exempt from the duty of chastity, Hume explains that the degree of the duty is far weaker for men than for women. Men, Hume explains, should not have "*entire* liberty of indulging their appetites in venereal enjoyment," but women are expected not only to be at all times chaste, but even to experience repugnance at even the slightest expression of "liberty."[93]

Hume argues that this double standard concerning chastity, although a "voluntary convention," is in the interest of society and thus is an artificial virtue. He bases the necessity of the stricter rule of chastity for women upon the biological fact that proof of parenthood is more difficult for a man to acquire than for a woman. Pointing to the "length and feebleness of human infancy" and positing a natural concern for one's offspring, Hume concludes that there must be a union of "considerable duration" of the parents of a child. He argues that "in order to induce the men to impose on themselves this restraint, and undergo cheerfully all the fatigues and expenses, to which it subjects them, they must believe, that the children are their own, and that their natural instinct is not directed to a wrong object."[94]

Hume's argument in support of the stricter rule of chastity for women is based on a number of presuppositions. For instance, he assumes the financial dominance of men. If resources were primarily in the possession of women, or if women had a good share of such resources, unions of considerable duration as envisioned by Hume would not be necessary. However, since men's financial dominance was the social condition of eighteenth-century Europe, it was consistent for Hume to assume it. Hume goes on to make two additional presuppositions concerning human nature: (1) that a man would be willing to offer economic support to a child only if he knew that he was that child's biological father, and (2) that women, even more than men, are apt to succumb to the temptations of sex. The first presupposition is highly questionable, but it is the second that is the concern of my discussion.

In his discussion of chastity, Hume again expresses his belief that woman is more susceptible than man to the passions of love. In detailing the nature of the rule of chastity for women, Hume insists that the punishment of bad fame or reputation and the praise of chastity, although motives to fidelity, would not be sufficient to insure the chastity of women. "All human creatures, *especially of the female sex*, are apt to over-look remote motives in favour of any present temptation: The temptation is here the strongest imaginable."[95] Hume's double standard concerning the artificial virtue of chastity is thus directly related to his beliefs concerning woman's weakness of mind. It is because of woman's weakness of mind that she is more likely to succumb to the amorous passions and less capable of properly judging the utility of an action. Hume concludes that the chastity of woman is assured only if "beside the infamy attending such licenses, there shou'd be some preceding backwardness or dread, which may prevent their first approaches, and may give the female sex a repugnance to all expressions, and postures, and liberties, that have an immediate relation to that enjoyment."[96] And this is to be assured through education. Thus Hume, like Rousseau and Kant, argues that it is for the good of mankind that the education of woman be different from that of man, for it must instill in the "ductile minds of the fair sex" a repugnance of infidelity. I believe it not unreasonable to suppose that the type of education required to impose upon woman an abhorrence of infidelity would be in tension with the type of intellectual education needed to develop the courage and insight of a Cleanthes.*

Thus it appears that Hume's selection of a man to represent the moral person is not an accident. Woman's natural inferiority constitutes an impediment to moral action, an impediment some, but not all, women can to some extent overcome.† A woman will be less capable of accurate judgment, and thus more likely to be in error concerning the utility of an action. A woman

---

* This was certainly the conclusion of Rousseau, and we know that Hume was very influenced by his ideas.

† Given Hume's belief in the superiority of European peoples over all others, there is good reason to conclude that he would deny that nonwhite women were capable of overcoming their natural inferiorities of both race and sex.

will be less capable of resisting present temptations and holding to more remote interests, especially if the former involve sex. We do not find chastity among the list of the virtues of Cleanthes, yet Hume would place chastity at the top of the list of the virtues of woman. Thus although Hume's moral theory, unlike Kant's, offers a characterization of the ideal moral person as possessing both feminine and masculine traits, we are forced to the conclusion that the Humean moral person is still gendered, that is, is male, and, once again, a "civilized" one.

This conclusion receives additional support from an examination of Hume's descriptions of virtuous women. It is particularly revealing that when Hume does praise a woman as a person of virtue, he sees her as having overcome the traits "natural to her sex" and describes her as masculine. For example, Jaqueline, countess of Hainault and Holland, is described as "a princess of a masculine spirit and uncommon understanding."[97] Hume tells us that Joan of Arc "never betrayed any weakness or womanish submission" during her interrogations. And in judging the reign of Elizabeth we are told not to "contemplate her as a woman," but rather "as a rational being placed in authority." If we do so, Hume concludes that "we may find it difficult to reconcile our fancy to her as a wife or a mistress; but her qualities as a sovereign, though with some considerable exceptions, are the object of undisputed applause and approbation."[98]

Although I do believe that Hume unquestioningly accepted the sexist bias of his eighteenth-century European culture involving woman's innate inferiority, I do not find his moral theory to be inherently sexist or androcentric. That is, his moral theory, unlike that of Kant, does not privilege traits historically viewed as masculine. It rather characterizes the moral individual as possessing a blend of traits typically considered feminine and masculine. Furthermore, Hume's moral theory is founded upon a concern for the relations between people, and, in particular, familial relations, again a characteristic historically classified as feminine. Hume's perception of woman's lesser participation in the moral realm is not inherent to the structure of his moral theory, but rather arises from his supposition of woman's inherent weakness of mind being superimposed upon his theory of morality, a bias that could be removed without radical changes to his moral theory.* In other words, the gendering of the Humean moral person that I have demonstrated above is not a necessary consequence of Hume's moral system. One can thus find in Hume's moral theory an example of a gender-neutral theory. But we

---

* I believe there is a subtle privileging of the emotions in Hume's theory, many of those he associates with woman's nature being viewed as antithetical to moral agency. But I believe this bias could be removed with relatively minor "tinkering" and would not require transforming the basic structure of Hume's moral theory.

also learn from Hume an important lesson—a gender-neutral moral theory is not sufficient for the full inclusion of women in the moral realm.

∾❧∽

My initial prediction that women would fare better with a moral theory like that of Hume, which incorporates the emotions, than with one like Kant's, which excludes emotion from the moral realm, was erroneous. Despite significant differences in their moral theory, Kant and Hume hold surprisingly similar positions concerning woman's moral capabilities. Hume's theory appears to be a bit more favorable to women than does Kant, since Kant holds that women are incapable of moral agency, while Hume holds the milder tenet that they are less capable of acting morally than men. While Hume viewed woman's innate traits as an impediment to her moral agency, Kant excluded woman from the moral realm not because of her nature, but because of his belief that the development of woman's rational capacities would impede man's moral development.

Kant's philosophy excludes women in a variety of different ways. I have shown that we must give an affirmative answer to each of my initial questions when they are applied to Kantian moral theory: Kantian morality is male. Women, on Kant's reckoning, are incapable of moral agency. Characteristics of the Kantian moral person privilege traits traditionally viewed as masculine. Kant believes that the source of a good woman's actions is different than that of a good man's. Finally, for Kant, the attainment of moral agency involves the complete mastery of traits perceived as feminine.

Answering these questions concerning Hume's moral theory is more complex. To the first question, "Is morality male?" I must answer both no and yes. I have argued that Humean moral theory is androgynous, including stereotypically feminine emotion as well as stereotypically masculine reason and being concerned with relationships between people. Thus, Hume's moral theory is not male, for it does not privilege traits historically associated with males. However, Hume's moral person is male. Despite Hume's inclusion of traits historically considered feminine in his description of the moral individual, Hume believed that woman's nature, in particular her sexual nature, would present a greater impediment to moral action than would man's nature. Unlike Kant, Hume does not believe that the source of a good woman's actions would be different than that of man's. For Hume, there is no difference between the moral action of a woman and of a man. The difference is rather that Hume believed that a woman would be less likely to act morally than a man. Hume thus presents us with the interesting combination of a theory which includes traits traditionally viewed as feminine within the moral realm but denies to the majority of women a fully developed moral capacity. Despite the promise of Hume's moral theory from a feminist perspective, a careful examination of his philosophy reminds us of the significance of the impact of an Aristotelian view of woman's natural inferiority.

We also learn an important lesson from Kant concerning the tension, previously noted with Descartes, between, on the one hand, defining reason and morality solely in terms of traits historically accepted as masculine and, on the other, the roles and characteristics socially ascribed to women. The very inconsistencies I noted in Kant's theory—his acceptance of the duty of self-perfection, but his denial that woman should develop their rational faculties; his acknowledgment of the practical imperative, while treating woman as a means—arise out of this tension. The Kantian acceptance of a Rousseauean view of the importance of the complementarity of the sexes, coupled with a definition of the moral individual which involves only masculine traits, makes the full moral enfranchisement of women impossible.

But even if Kant had not subscribed to this tenet, his moral theory would still be problematic for women. Given the fact that the characteristics Kant uses to define the moral individual are historically seen as masculine, a woman attempting to position herself within Kantian moral theory must deny in herself all those traits historically considered feminine. That is, to be a moral individual, a woman must become like a man. This sets up an obvious tension for women, a tension made greater by the commonly held Aristotelian view of natural differences between the sexes and the view that these differences dictate different social roles. A moral theory that privileges traits historically viewed as masculine will cause men and women alike to conclude that it is more difficult for a woman to be moral than for a man. A European woman of the eighteenth century inherited a cultural perception of woman as less capable than her male counterpart of the detached rationality mandated by Kant. Furthermore, her social roles, especially motherhood as it was defined in the eighteenth century, encouraged the development of the very characteristics she must repress in order to act morally. Thus, Kant embraces two tenets that exclude women from the moral realm: his premise of the complementarity of the sexes and the maleness of his definition of moral agency.

Kant, like many other philosophers, strongly believed that women's and men's roles must be different. Some, like Kant and Rousseau, believed that the complementarity of gender roles was a prerequisite for the good society. Other philosophers pointed to woman's natural inferiority to man as justification for different social roles. Regardless of the reason, the common conclusion was that woman is best suited for the private realm and only man is capable of full participation of the public realm. It is to such theories that I will now turn.

FURTHER READINGS

Primary Texts

KANT

Anthropology from a Pragmatic Point of View, Part Two, B (The Character of the Sexes)

Grounding for the Metaphysics of Morals, especially the first and second sections

The Metaphysical Principles of Virtue

Observations on the Feeling of the Beautiful and Sublime, Section Three (Of the Distinction of the Beautiful and Sublime in the Interrelations of the Two Sexes); see also Section Four (Of National Characteristics)

HUME

Enquiry Concerning the Principles of Morals, Section II, "Of Benevolence"; section III, "Of Justice"; section IX, "Conclusion"; appendix I, "Concerning Moral Sentiment"

Essays, "Of Essay Writing," "Of Love and Marriage," "On the Immortality of the Soul," "On National Characters," "On Polygamy and Divorces," "On the Rise and Progress of the Arts and Sciences"

A Treatise of Human Nature, Book II, part II, section III, "Of the Amorous Passions, or Love betwixt the Sexes"; book II, part III, section III, "Of the Influencing Motives of the Will"; book III, part II, section XII, "Of Chastity and Modesty"

Secondary Texts

KANT AND WOMAN/THE FEMININE

Cartwright, David. "Kant's View of the Moral Significance of Kindhearted Emotions and the Moral Insignificance of Kant's View." *The Journal of Value Inquiry* 21 (1987): 291–304.

Gould, Timothy. "Engendering Aesthetics: Sublimity, Sublimation and Misogyny in Burke and Kant." In *Aesthetics, Politics, and Hermeneutics*. Ed. Gerald Bruns and Stephen Watson. Albany: State University of New York Press, 1991.

———. "Intensity and Its Audiences: Notes towards a Feminist Perspective on the Kantian Sublime." *The Journal of Aesthetics and Art Criticism* 48, 4 (1990): 305–315.

Korsgaard, Christine M. "Kant's Formula of Humanity." *Kantstudien* 77 (1986): 183–202.

Lloyd, Genevieve. *The Man of Reason: "Male" and "Female" in Western*

Philosophy. Minneapolis: University of Minnesota Press, 1984. Chapter 4.

Mendus, Susan. "Kant: An Honest but Narrow-Minded Bourgeois?" In *Women in Western Political Philosophy: Kant to Nietzsche*. Eds. Ellen Kennedy and Susan Mendus. New York: St. Martin's Press, 1987. Pp. 21–43.

Rumsey, Jean P. "The Development of Character in Kantian Moral Theory." *Journal of the History of Philosophy* XXVII, 2 (1989): 247–265.

Schott, Robin May. *Cognition and Eros: A Critique of the Kantian Paradigm*. Boston: Beacon Press, 1988.

HUME AND WOMAN/THE FEMININE

Baier, Annette C. "Good Men's Women: Hume on Chastity and Trust," *Hume Studies* V (1979): 1–19.

———. "Hume, The Women's Moral Theorist?" *Women and Moral Theory*. Eds. Eva Feder Kittay and Diana T. Meyers. Savage, MD: Rowman & Littlefield, 1987.

Bar-On, Bat Ami. "Could There Be a Humean Sex-Neutral General Idea of Man?" *Philosophy Research Archives* XIII (1987–88): 367–377.

Battersby, Christine. "An Enquiry Concerning the Humean Woman." *Philosophy* 56 (1981): 303–312.

Burns, Steven A. Macleod. "The Humean Female." In *The Sexism of Social and Political Theory: Women and Reproduction from Plato to Nietzsche*. Eds. Lorenne M. G. Clark and Lynda Lange. Toronto: University of Toronto Press, 1979.

Lacoste, Louise Marcil. "Hume's Method in Moral Reasoning." In *The Sexism of Social and Political Theory: Women and Reproduction from Plato to Nietzsche*. Eds. Lorenne M. G. Clark and Lynda Lange. Toronto: University of Toronto Press, 1979.

———. "Hume's Position Concerning Women." *Dialogue* 15 (1976): 425–440.

Lind, Marcia. "Indians, Savages, Peasants, and Women: Hume's Aesthetics." In *Critical Feminist Essays*. Ed. Bat Ami Bar-On. State University of New York Press, forthcoming 1991.

Lloyd, Genevieve. *The Man of Reason: "Male" and "Female" in Western Philosophy*. Minneapolis: University of Minnesota Press, 1984. Chapter 3.

WOMEN AND MORAL THEORY

Andolsen, Barbara Hilkert, Christine E. Gudorf, and Mary D. Pellauer, eds. *Women's Consciousness, Women's Conscience: A Reader in Feminist Ethics*. New York: Winston Press, 1985.

Brabeck, Mary, ed. *Who Cares? Theory, Research, and Educational Implications of the Ethics of Care*. New York, Prager, 1989.

Gilligan, Carol. *In a Different Voice: Psychological Theory and Women's Development*. Cambridge: Harvard University Press, 1982.

Held, Virginia. *Rights and Goods: Justifying Social Action*. New York: Free Press, 1984.

Hoagland, Sarah Lucia. *Lesbian Ethics: Toward New Value*. Palo Alto, CA: Institute of Lesbian Studies, 1988.

Kittay, Eva Feder, and Diana T. Meyers, eds. *Women and Moral Theory*. Savage, MD: Rowman & Littlefield, 1987.

Mattick, Paul, Jr. "Beautiful and Sublime: Gender Totemism in the Constitution of Art." *The Journal of Aesthetics and Art Criticism* 48, 4 (1990): 293–303.

Noddings, Nel. *Caring: A Feminine Approach to Ethics and Moral Education*. Berkeley: University of California Press, 1984.

Ruddick, Sara. *Maternal Thinking: Toward a Politics of Peace*. Boston: Beacon Press, 1989.

WOMEN IN EIGHTEENTH-CENTURY ENGLAND AND GERMANY

Hill, Bridget. *Eighteenth-Century Women: An Anthology*. Boston: Allen and Unwin, 1984.

Joeres, Ruth-Ellen B. *German Women in the Eighteenth and Nineteenth Century: A Social and Literary History*. Bloomington: Indiana University Press, 1986.

Meyers, Sylvia Harcstark. *The Bluestocking Circle: Women, Friendship, and the Life of the Mind in Eighteenth-Century England*. Oxford: Clarendon Press, 1990.

Mobius, Helga. *Woman of the Baroque Age*. Trans. Barbara Chruscick Beedham. Montclair, NJ: Allanheld & Schram, 1984.

Prior, Mary, ed. *Women in English Society 1500–1800*. New York: Methuen, 1985.

CHAPTER FIVE

THE PRIVATIZED WOMAN

With the exception of Plato, Western philosophers developing social or political theory unquestioningly accepted the division between the public realm of politics and citizenry and the private realm of familial relations. They saw the public realm, involving the power of ruling over others, as the arena of the rational and thus limited it to those who were superior in reason and virtue. In turn, they considered those relegated to the private realm as capable only of a limited and inferior virtue, and labeled them the "naturally ruled." Although defining the private realm as inferior in essence, intent, and purpose to the public realm, they looked upon it as providing the foundation, both productively and reproductively, upon which the public realm rests.

Until the end of the Middle Ages, the placing of individuals in their "appropriate" realm is justified by the assumption of either a natural or a divinely designed hierarchy of perfection. Free women, slaves, and children, being inferior to free men, can be logically excluded from participation in public life. Only the free adult male is capable of action within both the private and the public realm. Only he is capable of the rationality and morality necessary for participation in the public voice, qualities which also justify his serving as the ruler of his family. Thus all women, both free and slave, are to be subjected to the rule of free men. Women cannot participate in the public realm or rule in the private.

This assumption of a hierarchy of being begins to be challenged in the seventeenth century. Theorists such as Hobbes and Locke, and, in the eighteenth century, Bentham and Mill, reject the previous world view and argue rather for the premise of the natural equality and freedom of human beings. According to this nascent liberal theory, no individual possesses natural authority over another. Liberalists view all individuals in the original state of nature as free and equal. Relations of authority are thus not naturally ordained, but can be established only by rational consent.

Hobbes and Locke are among the first political theorists to question patriarchal political theory: the view that the father possesses natural and unlimited authority over the family and that this natural authority is the basis for monarchical power. According to patriarchal theory, the father, given sole credit for causing the generation of his children and granted authority over his wife via God's original covenant with Adam, possesses sovereignty over his family. Such familial relations are then seen as the paradigm for political relations. In this way, the king, as the father of his people, is credited with divinely ordained sovereignty over them. Thus authority is natural and hierarchical.

The debates between liberalism and paternalism rest upon the controversy over natural versus rational authority. Paternalism, with its emphasis on scriptural justifications of women's subordination to their husbands, precludes a position of sexual equality. But the liberal belief in the natural equality of all individuals opens the door to sexual as well as racial equality. Liberal theorists cannot consistently hold that *all* individuals are free and equal in the state of nature and support a relation of natural authority of husbands over wives.

I will limit my analysis of liberal theory to that of John Locke (1632–1704).[1] I will argue that the prejudice of woman's natural inferiority and the strength of the belief in the necessity of man's having authority over her was so powerful that Locke was unable to accept the implications of his own liberal arguments.

THE FORCE OF PREJUDICE: LOCKE

In developing his theory of authority, Locke is consciously attacking patriarchalism in general and the theory of his contemporary Sir Robert Filmer in particular. Since much of Locke's own theory is framed in opposition to that of Filmer, it is helpful to begin with an overview of the latter's defense of patriarchy.

Filmer's intent is to demonstrate that a monarch's claim to absolute rule is divinely sanctioned. The strength of Filmer's theory derives from the fact that he bases it on two sources of authority that are widely respected in the seventeenth century: scripture and the patriarchal family experience.

Filmer turns to Genesis to prove that the rule of husband over wife and children is divinely ordained, as well as to establish the divine grant of monarchical power to Adam. It is Filmer's claim that Adam is given rule over his wife and over nature from the moment of creation. Filmer focuses his scriptural arguments for monarchy on proving that

God gave to Adam not only the dominion over the woman and the children that should issue from them, but also over the whole earth to subdue it, and over all the creatures on it, so that as long as Adam lived no man could claim or enjoy anything but by donation, assignation, or permission from him.[2]

By then tracing the king's power back to Adam, the original "monarch of the whole world," Filmer argues that the king's claim to absolute rule is divinely ordained.

Filmer's position is also rooted in the patriarchal family experience of the seventeenth century. The seventeenth-century family was unambiguously ruled by the father. The family was a central focus of life, and the father was accepted as possessing immense power. By grounding the power of the monarch in the already accepted power of the father, Filmer was able to further strengthen his patriarchal theory. The king, as father, was to provide for, instruct, and defend his people, who were in turn to give him their complete obedience.[3]

To successfully support the position that all individuals are naturally equal and free, Locke must refute both of the above cornerstones of Filmer's argument for natural authority. My focus here will be on Locke's arguments concerning women. I will show that although Locke disputes Filmer's tenet that God gave Adam dominion over Eve upon her creation as well as his claim of the absolute authority of the father, Locke does not deny that women are to be in subjection to men.

Locke clearly identifies the weak point of Filmer's scriptural arguments concerning man's dominion over woman. He notes that the original grant given by God in Genesis 1:28 was spoken in the plural "them": "And God blessed them [male and female], and God said to them, 'Be fruitful and multiply, and fill the earth and subdue it; and have dominion over the fish of the sea and over the birds of the air and over every living thing that moves upon the earth.' " Locke interprets this to mean that God gave dominion to the human species since, being made in God's image, they were intelligent creatures and thus capable of dominion.[4] On this interpretation, dominion is given both to woman and to man. Locke concludes that even if man receives divinely sanctioned authority over woman, it cannot be absolute. "If it be said that *Eve* was subjected to *Adam*, it seems she was not so subjected to him, as to hinder her *Dominion* over the Creatures, or *Property* in them."[5]

Locke also addresses God's curse saying that Eve's desire should be for her husband and that he would rule over her. Locke carefully points out that given that both Adam and Eve have disobeyed God's command, this curse was not designed to be a grant of privilege to Adam. Locke thus denies Filmer's claim that these words contain "the original grant of government." Instead Locke argues that they "at most concern the Female Sex only, and import no more but that Subjection they should ordinarily be in to their Husbands."[6] Locke sees the curse not as establishing woman's subordination to her husband, but rather as predicting it. Nor does Locke think this "ordinary" subjection need be the same for all women, for the "Circumstances either of her Condition or Contract with her Husband" can exempt a woman from it.[7] Locke concludes that Filmer's claim that a husband's authority over his wife is divinely sanctioned is not supported by scripture. "God, in this Text, gives not, that I see, any Authority to *Adam* over *Eve*, or to Men over their Wives, but only foretels what should be the Womans Lot."[8]

Although we might expect, given his liberal tenet of the original equality of all people, that Locke would conclude from his analysis of Genesis that woman is to be man's equal, he does not. After arguing that God's curse on Eve is not to be interpreted as a divine sanction of a woman's subjection to her husband, he does admit that there is "a Foundation in Nature for it."[9] Locke does not disclose what constitutes this foundation, but simply assumes that his reader will accept his claim and moves on to an analysis of the specific nature of a wife's subordination to her husband.

Although it is impossible to know why Locke simply asserts woman's natural inferiority and quickly moves on to the next issue, it is possible to speculate on the question. A belief in the natural inferiority of women would have been generally accepted by a seventeenth-century readership, so Locke may not have seen it as in need of elaboration or justification. Still, such a tenet creates a tension within Locke's general political philosophy, a tension he is aware of and attempts to address. In order to discuss the nature of this tension, I will first turn to Locke's theory of political authority and, in particular, his vision of the state of nature.

Locke is concerned to refute patriarchalism's view of authority as a natural relation. Locke's position is that legitimate political authority is not divinely ordained, but is based on voluntary consent, what he calls the social contract. Authority then is not a natural relationship, but a rational relationship. Locke insists that in order to "understand Political Power right, and derive it from its Original, we must consider what State all Men are naturally in."[10] According to Locke, this state of nature is one in which all individuals are equal and free. This freedom consists in an individual's "*Liberty* to dispose, and order, as he lists, his Person, Actions, Possessions, and his whole Property, within the Allowance of those Laws under which he is; and therein not to be subject to the arbitrary Will of another, but freely follow his own."[11] These laws are the laws of reason; to abandon the use of one's reason is to violate the laws of nature. Because all adult individuals are "furnished with like Faculties, sharing all in one Community of Nature, there cannot be supposed any such *Subordination* among us."[12]

But what of women and their subordination, when married, to their husbands? If the state of nature is one in which there is no subordination between individuals, are we to assume that Locke did not see conjugal relations as occurring within the state of nature? Or was the marriage relationship different in the state of nature than in the political state? The questions make clear the tension between Locke's view of woman's natural inferiority and his political philosophy.

Locke is not unaware of this tension. Concerned to deny that political authority is grounded in paternal relations, Locke is careful to argue that political and conjugal authority are different. The power of a husband over his wife, Locke explains, "can be only a Conjugal Power . . . but not a Political Power of Life and Death over her."[13] Locke views marriage as a contractual relationship, "made by a voluntary Compact between Man and Woman."[14] But the relationship between husband and wife is, for Locke, a blend of natural and contractual elements.

The initial decision to marry is an issue of choice, according to Locke, and is one in which women retain some latitude. Locke tells us that a woman is free to negotiate for a better marriage contract, and allows even that her circumstances, as in the case of queens, might mitigate her subjection. Still, Locke perceives the chief end of marriage as procreation and argues that this element carries with it natural elements of authority in the relationship between wife and husband.

Locke rejects Filmer's position that procreation gave the father absolute authority over his children. Locke reasons that the relation of begetting referred to by Filmer as conferring absolute authority on the father would actually only "give the *Father* but a joynt Dominion with the Mother over them. For no body can deny but that the Woman hath an equal share . . . in begetting of the Child."[15] Locke agrees with Filmer that procreation creates a natural relation of authority but argues, contrary to Filmer, that the relation of authority accrues to the mother and the father equally. Thus Locke undercuts Filmer's foundation for the patriarchal monarch.

Since children are born weak and helpless, Locke holds that by law of nature all parents are *"under an obligation to preserve, nourish, and educate the Children*, they had begotten."[16] This natural duty carries a relation of authority, since parents must direct and guide their children. Locke would thus agree with Filmer that familial relations include natural powers, but insists that "in this power the *Mother* too has her share with the *Father*."[17]

It would be an error, however, to conclude that Locke viewed the role of mother and father as equal. Locke argues that the nourishment and maintenance of children requires a "Community of Goods," or family property. Locke defines this fact as carrying a second natural element into the conjugal relationship, and it is this element which results in the subordination of the wife to the husband. Arguing that a wife and husband will have different understandings and thus different wills, Locke insists that rule over family property must be limited to one of them. "It therefore being necessary, that the last Determination, i.e. the Rule, should be placed somewhere, it naturally falls to the Man's share, as the abler and the stronger."[18] Locke thus reiterates his belief in woman's natural inferiority and uses it as a foundation for supporting the necessary subordination of a woman to her husband concerning the disposition of the family property.*

Thus although the conjugal relationship originates as a consensual relationship, its aim, procreation, carries with it natural duties to children, which require property held in common. This in conjunction with man's "natural superiority" endows the husband with an additional source of nonconsensual authority, for it is he who will control the distribution of all common property. Thus Locke views the typical marriage as a consensual arrangement in which a woman agrees to surrender control of family property to her husband. In this way, Locke attempts to resolve the apparent tension between his thesis that political authority is consensual and his belief that the wife is to be ruled by her husband. Conjugal authority is, in nature and source, different from political authority. Locke explains that conjugal power includes "the Power that every Husband hath to order the things of private Concernment in his Family, as Proprietor of the Goods and Land there, and to have his Will take place before that of his wife in all things of their common Concernment."[19]

The force of prejudice in Locke's theory is apparent at this point. Not only does he unquestioningly accept the centuries-old belief in woman's biological inferiority, he views it as entailing the subordination of a woman to her husband within the marriage relationship, thus forcing him to posit a problematic type of power, conjugal power. Conjugal power, like political power, is a contractual relationship. But conjugal power is not absolute as is political power. As we have seen, Locke clearly denies a husband the power of life and death over his wife. But the conjugal relationship is not purely consensual for Locke, for there is also a natural element, namely the natural subordination of wife to husband concerning family property. Thus conjugal power is neither fully consensual, as is political power, nor fully natural, as is parental power, but an awkward mix of the two.

Locke's prejudice is further revealed if we look at his position concerning the significance of natural differences between individuals in regard to political power. Here Locke clearly acknowledges that there are natural differences between individuals.

---

* Locke follows his claim that the husband is to have authority over common property with the qualification that this authority does not include any property a woman retained sole rights over via the specifics of her marriage contract. He reiterates his claim that a woman can strive to procure the most favorable contract, that is, keep rights over property she owns or will inherit. Nevertheless, this passage casts doubt on his earlier claim that in the most favorable circumstances (e.g., queens) a woman can be exempted from subjection to her husband (*Two Treatises of Government*, ed. Peter Laslett [New York: Cambridge University Press, 1963], I, 47). It appears that even the most favorable marriage contract cannot preclude the authority of the husband over interests in common to the family.

Age or *Virtue* may give Men a just Precedency: *Excellency of Parts and Merit* may place others above the Common Level: *Birth* may subject some, and *Alliance* or *Benefits* others, to pay an Observance to those to whom Nature, Gratitude or other Respects may have made it due; and yet all this consists with the *Equality* which all Men are in, in respect of Jurisdiction or Dominion one over another.[20]

Locke is clear in insisting that equality in respect of jurisdiction or dominion does not require "sameness." Yet he concludes that the alleged natural differences between women and men dictate a subordination of wives to husbands. Despite the tension between these views, Locke gives no reason why the greater strength or ability of a husband should require the subjection of his wife.

In Locke's philosophy, the right to autonomy overrides differences in abilities between men, but natural differences between the sexes, except in exceptional cases, override this right. Yet we are provided no explanation for this disparity other than the unsupported assertion that rule must be limited to one person to avoid differences in understanding or wills. It appears that not all individuals are free and equal, even in the state of nature. Men's autonomy is absolute and not relative to their individual abilities. Not so with women's autonomy. Once a woman consents to marriage, natural differences limit her right to autonomy and result in a justified subordination of her will to that of her husband.

The question now arises as to the impact of this conjugal authority. That is, does woman's subordinate role in the family affect her potential for action and authority within the political realm? To answer this question, we must return to Locke's account of the origin of government. In the words of Teresa Brennan and Carole Pateman, we must not forget that "Locke's state of nature contains government—the government of the fathers."[21] But if we examine his position carefully, we find that the above-mentioned tensions are not in fact resolved.

Locke argues that the form of government which limits rule to one person originated in the family. Looking back to the state of nature, Locke speculates that without any rule, it would have been hard for people to live together. He claims that it is likeliest that this rule "should, by the express or tacit Consent of the Children, when they were grown up, be in the Father."[22] He argues that a monarchical government arose out of this experience. That is, Locke suggests that "the Father's Government of the Childhood of those sprung from him "accustomed them to the *Rule of one Man*."[23] When individuals joined together to form a society, it was natural for them, given this earlier experience, to "chuse the wisest and bravest Man to conduct them in their Wars, and lead them out against their Enemies, and in this chiefly be their *Ruler*."[24] Although this sounds like Filmer's position, it is actually different, because the cause of the genesis of such rule is not natural or divine law, but rather custom and habit.

This account of the origins of government is, however, in tension with Locke's view of conjugal relations. According to Locke, the mother and the father *together* have authority over the children. The government of childhood thus is not "the rule of one man," but of two people. Locke cannot base an argument for the origins of government on *paternal* authority, for in his attempt to undercut Filmer's argument for patriarchalism, Locke has replaced paternal authority with parental authority.* How then can Locke support his view that the children, when grown, would from habit consent to the rule of the father? If we look closely at Locke's account, we find that the authority of the father over the children is more extensive than that of the mother.

The only area of conjugal life over which the father possesses sole dominion is the disposition of common property. Locke views this power of the father as typically resulting in a stronger bond of obedience to him than to the mother and thus as a source of paternal authority. "There is *another Power* ordinarily *in the Father*, whereby he has a tie on the Obedience of his Children. . . . And this is the Power Men generally have to *bestow their Estates* on those, who please them best."[25] Locke perceives this power as resulting in an important tie to the obedience of his children which lasts even when they are no longer minors.

The only chance for a woman to have the power to bestow property is if through negotiation in her marriage contract she retains rights to her own property. "The Wife [is] in the full and free possession of what by Contract is her peculiar Right."[26] Locke allows that a woman could own property not subject to her husband's control. Such a woman would be able to determine which child inherits her property and would thereby have a bond of obedience similar to that of the father, who would still retain the power to dispose of common property. But Locke perceived only the exceptional woman to be capable of this option. Thus it is his view that in the typical case, paternal authority would be stronger than maternal authority; the basis again is Locke's insistence that the man, being by nature abler and stronger, possesses conjugal authority.

The question here arises as to the relation between women and civil society in Locke's political theory. Locke argues that "the great and *chief end* . . . of Mens uniting into Commonwealths, and putting themselves under Government, is the *Preservation of their Property*."[27] Thus Locke tells us that

---

* Locke, however, is not always consistent in this. For example, in discussing the duty to educate children, Locke refers to it as a paternal power. *Two Treatises*, II (Ibid., 69).

humans, being rational individuals, agree to establish civil society and thereby surrender much of their power in order to receive the protection of their property. But in the typical marriage contract, women consent to forfeit control over their property or any common property. So if property constitutes the primary reason for entering into civil society, it begins to appear that women (as well as propertyless men) will benefit less from civil society than propertied men. Is there thus an elitism and sexism in Locke's political philosophy which precludes women and men without property from full participation in the civil state?

In fairness to Locke, it has been noted that his use of the term "property" is somewhat vague.[28] In his long discussion of property in the *Second Treatise* he limits its meaning to land and goods. Since we are to assume from Locke's account that in the typical marriage contract a woman's right to property is waived, control of conjugal property being in the hands of her husband, woman will have little interest in entering into the social contract if the function of government is construed as protecting land and goods. In other places Locke defines property as life, liberty, and estate. But even broadening the role of government to include the protection of property in this expanded sense, women would typically benefit *less* than propertied men, for the average woman would have less direct interest in the protection of property than would her husband. Given this description of government, civil society can thus be seen as providing a continuum of benefits to its members. All individuals benefit equally from governmental protection of life. And all, whether rich or poor, are equally subject to the law. But the benefits concerning protection of material property accrue more to some individuals than to others. Those with the most property have the most to lose and thus benefit the most from governmental protection of lands and goods. On Locke's account, only slaves are exempt from civil society, for they have "forfeited their Lives, and with it their Liberties, and lost their Estates; and being in the *State of Slavery*, not capable of any Property, cannot in that state be considered as any part of *Civil Society*; the chief end whereof is the preservation of Property."[29]

The impact of the typical marriage contract in which a woman consents to have the family property ruled by her husband is broadened by examining Locke's views on the relationship between property and rationality. Here Locke's views on laborers are revealing. C. B. Macpherson argues that Locke's remarks on wage-laborers indicate a belief that their life-style precludes their ability to develop their rational capacities. Locke claims that the income of laborers, "being seldom more than a bare subsistence, never allows that body of men time or opportunity to raise their thoughts above that."[30] It seems that Locke, like Plato and Aristotle before him, believes that leisure is required for the development of rationality.

The greatest part of mankind have not leisure for learning and logic, and superfine distinctions of the schools. Where the hand is used to the plough and the spade, the head is seldom elevated to sublime notions, or exercised in mysterious reasoning. It is well if men of that rank (to say nothing of the other sex) can comprehend plain propositions, and a short reasoning about things familiar to their minds, and nearly allied to their daily experience. Go beyond this, and you amaze the greatest part of mankind. . . .[31]

Although Locke accepted the tenet that in the state of nature, people* are by nature equally rational, subsequent decisions concerning labor and property resulted in differences in the development of their rational capacities. This variation would manifest itself as a class difference, since those who were laborers would not be able to develop their rational capacities through industrious appropriation of property. In addition, since individuals enter into the social contract in order to protect property, laborers who are thus without property will not be full members of civil society. As explained by Macpherson, "only those with 'estate' can be full members, for two reasons: only they have a full interest in the preservation of property, and only they are fully capable of that rational life—that voluntary obligation to the law of reason—which is the necessary basis of full participation in civil society."[32]

Clearly there is a classism in Locke's philosophy, but what of sexism? Of course, 50 percent of the laborers are women and are thus precluded from a rational life. But women of the propertied class, even those of a typical marriage in which the husband controls the property, still presumably have the leisure for development of their rational capacities. In fact in a letter to a woman friend concerning the education of her daughter, Locke wrote that he would "acknowledge no difference of sex in your mind relating . . . to truth, virtue, and obedience" and concluded that a young woman's education should be the same as that of a young man.[33]

Still for Locke there seems to be a connection between rationality and property.[34] The full development of rational capacities requires not only leisure but also property. Property does not simply allow for the leisure necessary for the development of rationality; it serves, for Locke, as the symbol of one's rational accomplishments. Being rational requires the ability to direct and control one's own life, which includes one's property. Laborers, having sold their labor to another, have lost control over their person and capacities. Another directs them. But consider even the upper-class woman. Although her person has not been alienated, if she has consented to the typical marriage contract, her property and the fruits of her labor have been alienated from

---

* Locke consistently says "men," but I will give him the benefit of the doubt.

her. She seems to be in a position midway between that of a propertied man and a laborer. Although she has the leisure to develop her rational capacities, she would not be able to use her rationality to direct and control property, and is in this way precluded from full membership in civil society. Only the exceptional woman who negotiates a nontypical marriage contract giving her property rights not subject to her husband's control is able to develop her rationality as fully as her husband.

The obvious question which arises from this analysis is why any woman would enter into what Locke considered to be the typical marriage contract, in which all property was subject to the authority of the husband. This question is particularly problematic given Locke's vision of the state of nature, in which all individuals are equal to each other so "there is no superiority or jurisdiction of one, over another" and all are free to "order their Actions, and dispose of their Possessions, and Persons as they think fit."[35] Since Locke has insisted that in regard to consent to the social contract, "no rational Creature can be supposed to change his condition with an intention to be worse," it is reasonable to assume that for him the same would hold of a woman's consent to a marriage contract.[36] Why then would a woman who is under no person's jurisdiction voluntarily place herself in subordination to a man?

As earlier discussed, Locke does acknowledge that not all women would consent to a marriage contract involving such subjection to their husbands. Referring to the Genesis statement of Eve's curse, Locke explains that "there is here no more Law to oblige a Woman to such a Subjection, if the Circumstances either of her Condition or Contract with her Husband should exempt her from it, then there is, that she should bring forth her Children in Sorrow and Pain, if there could be found a Remedy for it."[37] Locke does not dwell on this point, but offers an example that is problematic. He asks rhetorically whether "either of our Queens *Mary* or *Elizabeth*, had they Married any of their Subjects, had been by this Text put into a Political Subjection to him? or that he thereby should have had *Monarchical Rule* over her?"[38] Notice here that Locke equivocates. The primary form of subjection he refers to in this passage is "that Subjection they [wives] should ordinarily be in to their Husbands," that is, conjugal power. But when he mentions Queen Mary and Queen Elizabeth, he switches from conjugal power to political power. It is true that Mary's husband did not have political power over her, but since man is, on Locke's account, by nature "abler and stronger," it would follow that her husband should retain authority over family property. It is clear that Locke believed that the exceptional woman, the woman of royal blood or perhaps the woman who had inherited wealth, could use such circumstances to negotiate a marriage contract which gave her title to certain properties apart from the common goods and thus not subject to her husband's control.

It is less clear if we can interpret his position to include the belief that if a woman was exceptional enough, she could even negotiate a contract that precluded any kind of subordination to her husband. But let us concede to Locke the latter claim.

Granting this, let us ask the question again, Why in the state of nature where a woman is under no person's jurisdiction would the majority of women voluntarily give their consent to a marriage contract that placed them in subordination to their husbands? Locke seems to be of the opinion that individuals negotiate for the contract containing the most favorable terms; hence we are forced to conclude that Locke believed that the majority of women in the state of nature are not in a situation to negotiate a more favorable contract. The typical woman's choices are therefore limited, and marriage will result in her being without control of any property.

We are still left with the question as to just what it is about woman in the state of nature that typically precludes her ability to negotiate a more favorable marriage contract. Locke remains silent on this point; thus we are left to speculate. The most obvious conjecture is that Locke believed that woman's natural inferiority, what he termed her being "less strong and able," resulted in her being in an unfavorable position for negotiating a marriage contract. I would additionally conjecture that Locke, like generations of theorists before him, accepted the prevalent view that woman's role in procreation—her monthly cycles, the fact that it is she who gestates the fetus, and so on—constitutes a handicap which makes her dependent upon the support of a man and limits her ability to acquire or control property.* Thus the typical woman, having less property than the typical man and having a greater need for entering into a marriage relationship, would be forced to accept a marriage contract that included her subordination to her husband. Although Locke makes only fleeting reference to woman's natural inferiority to man, it appears that this tenet actually plays a more central role in his philosophy than might otherwise be acknowledged.

Although Locke's individualism allowed for the rise of the exceptional woman—the woman of royal blood and the propertied woman—the force of prejudice concerning gender permeated his political thought. Despite his liberalist political theory, his unquestioned assumption of woman's inferiority both justified and explained woman's subordination to her husband and made her role in the political realm problematic.

---

* This position, obviously, contains numerous biases concerning social structures (e.g., it assumes that the basic unit of the state of nature is the family) as well as depicts pregnancy as debilitating. But these views would have been consistent with Locke's seventeenth-century individualism.

THE PARADOX OF WOMAN: HEGEL

The admittedly problematic legacy of liberal theory's premise of the natural equality of all individuals did not eradicate the influence upon political theory of the belief in the complementarity of the sexes, a tenet clearly revived in the philosophy of Rousseau. The philosophy of Georg Wilhelm Friedrich Hegel (1770–1831) offers an illustration of a political theory which denies the liberal tenet of the equality of the sexes and rather embraces the belief that the roles and natures of women are different from, yet complementary to, those of men.

Like the majority of philosophers before him, Hegel accepts the division between the public realm of politics and citizenry and the private realm of familial relations. Hegel, however, perceives these two realms not as separate and unrelated, but rather as intimately connected through a series of dynamic relationships. Like Locke, Hegel rejects the patriarchalist tenet that authority relationships are uniform, the relationship between monarch and subjects mirroring that of father to children. According to Hegel, the modern social realm consists of three spheres—the family, civil society, and the state—each of which involves different social relationships. Hegel's views concerning the nature of these relationships and the respective roles of women and men arise out of his philosophical system.

Although space precludes an examination of the complexities of Hegel's system, an understanding of his views on the roles of women and men requires a general understanding of a few of his central tenets. In his *Phenomenology of Spirit*, Hegel offers an analysis of the emergence of reason in the human consciousness. He interprets this advance toward reason as requiring a more and more direct knowledge of objects, specifically, a knowing which progresses from consciousness to self-consciousness, to reason, and ultimately to what Hegel called "Spirit," or universal knowledge. This evolution occurs through a logic of the dialectic, in which the attempt to know something directly gives rise to contradictions between the world and our understanding of it, contradictions which are ultimately transcended and thereby engender more complete knowledge, until an understanding of the totality is achieved. The development of self-consciousness involves relations with others, since for Hegel self-consciousness requires recognition by another. The advance of reason thus requires the emergence of social life. Hegel details two moments in the evolution of social life: the pagan world and the modern world. It is in the course of this discussion that Hegel develops his views concerning the role of women.

Hegel places woman, whether pagan or modern, within the realm he labels the "*natural* Ethical community," the family.[39] Woman is thereby explicitly excluded from the political realm, but Hegel does not thereby conclude that woman's role is insubstantial or inconsequential. On the contrary, Hegel perceives the family as intimately connected to the state. It is not the romantic haven from the heartless sphere of the state. It is rather one of the "ethical root[s] of the state."⁴⁰ Therefore, to evaluate the role and position of woman in Hegel's philosophy, we must look closely at the nature of the Hegelian state.*

As noted earlier, Hegel perceives the modern state as consisting of the family, civil society, and the state. The family is indispensable, for it constitutes the first ethical relation in which one learns to be a member of a community which transcends individual persons. Civil society furthers this developing sense of community by allowing for the development of concrete personality through labor and fulfillment of need as well as through an enlarging sense of interdependence. The state, representing the most developed moment, is a synthesis of the family and civil society. Participation in the universal community of the state is the result of self-conscious choice rather than custom or instinct.

Since Hegel limits women to the first moment of ethical life, the family, I will focus initially on his discussion of the family. His first detailed description of the family and its relation to the state occurs in his work *The Phenomenology of Spirit*, in which he examines the nature of the family in the context of the Greek *polis*. He directs his second discourse on the family, published fourteen years later in his *Philosophy of Right*, to the modern family. To understand Hegel's philosophy concerning women, we must look at his views on both of these historical periods.

Hegel perceives the classical Greek society as divided into two realms: the family and the *polis*. Each realm embodies a different law—the family representing divine law, the *polis* representing human law. Nature, according to Hegel, assigns to woman the realm of divine law, to man the realm of human law. Human law, the law of the *polis*, enables man to defines himself through his identity with the community, that is, define himself as a citizen.†́ Human law is a "*known* law," "the form of a reality that is conscious of itself."⁴¹ Divine law, unlike human law, is not consciously known. It is "an implicit, inner essence which is not exposed to the daylight of consciousness,

---

* It is important to realize that in his discussion of the modern state, Hegel includes only European women and men. He has already precluded peoples of other nations from the modern state, arguing that they have yet to develop the idea of freedom which removes one's alienation from self through self-knowledge and self-determination, a condition necessary for participation in the Hegelian state. See, for example, his discussions of Africa and China as collected in his *Enzyklopadie der Philosophischen Wissenschaften im Grundriss*, Stuttgart: Frommann Verlag, 1956.

† The masculine pronoun here is intentional. As I will illustrate, Hegel precludes women from participation in the *polis*.

but remains an inner feeling and the divine element that is exempt from an existence in the real world."[42]

Just as the realms of the family and of the state are mutually dependent, so too are divine and human law. Woman, like man, is for Hegel an ethical being. Just as man enters into an ethical community when he identifies himself as a citizen, so too the family is an ethical whole in terms of which each member, including woman, defines her or his identity. Participation in the family as well as the state constitutes a relationship with the universal, and thus through such identification one enters the ethical realm.

In regard to the family, Hegel explains that

although the Family is *immediately* determined as an ethical being, it is within itself an *ethical* entity only so far as it is not the *natural* relationship of its members, or so far as their connection is an *immediate* connection of separate, actual individuals; for the ethical principle is intrinsically universal, and this natural relationship is just as much a spiritual one, and it is only as a spiritual entity that it is ethical.[43]

In other words, the ethical dimension of the family arises from an identity that is not a "natural" relationship, that is, according to Hegel, not one of feeling or the relationship of love. Rather, individuals must identify with the family itself, making the family rather than one's connections to particular individuals the end and content of one's actions. "It is not a question of *this* particular husband, *this* particular child, but simply of husband and children generally."[44] In this way one participates in the universal. Woman, thus, through her participation in the family, enters the ethical dimension.

Hegel, however, clearly perceives the law of the state, human law, as superior to that of the family, divine law. The scope of human law is the society as a whole, not simply the individual family. Man, through entrance into the *polis*, obtains knowledge of the universal. Woman, although possessing the highest *intuitive* awareness of what is ethical, does not attain to consciousness of it. It is human law that Hegel identifies with the universal spirit.

The Family, as the *unconscious*, still inner Notion [of the ethical order], stands opposed to its actual, self-conscious existence; as the *element* of the nation's actual existence, it stands opposed to the nation itself; as the *immediate* being of the ethical order, it stands over against that order which shapes and maintains itself by working for the universal; the Penates [household gods of blood and kinship] stand opposed to the universal Spirit.[45]

Human and divine law are interdependent in Hegel's scheme, but the former is clearly superior in being more universal. Woman, according to Hegel, is limited to the dialectically inferior realm of the family, while man, through his participation in the *polis*, "leaves this immediate, elemental, and therefore, strictly speaking, negative ethical life of the Family, in order to acquire and produce the ethical life that is conscious of itself and actual."[46]

The tragedy of the Greek world, according to Hegel, is the inevitable opposition of human and divine law. The realms, although interdependent, are also in tension, woman representing the law of the family, man the law of the state. Antigone's decision to bury Polyneices arises out of her familial duty to bury and honor her dead brother. Creon's decree that the traitor Polyneices be denied a burial represents the law of the state. Thus human law and divine law are set in opposition. According to Hegel, the tragedy represented in the *Antigone* results from the fact that the unmediated opposition of these two realms leads to the inescapable destruction of the pagan world. Woman, concerned with the law of the family, is seen by Hegel as being the catalyst of this destruction.

Since the community only gets an existence through its interference with the happiness of the Family, and by dissolving [individual] self-consciousness into the universal, it creates for itself in what it suppresses and what is at the same time essential to it an internal enemy—womankind in general. Womankind—the everlasting irony [in the life] of the community—changes by intrigue the universal end of the government into a private end.[47]

Hegel does not, in the *Phenomenology*, explain why woman is destined to be the irony of the community, that is, why she embodies the law of the divine, the law of the family, while man manifests the superior human law. To find the answer, we must look at Hegel's later writings, in particular his *Philosophy of Right* and his *Encyclopaedia of the Philosophical Sciences*.[48] Hegel justifies his exclusion of women from the state through recourse to very traditional-sounding arguments concerning biological differences between the sexes.

In the *Philosophy of Right*, Hegel explains that the "difference in the physical characteristics of the two sexes has a rational basis and consequently acquires an intellectual and ethical significance."[49] Like Rousseau before him, Hegel sees this rational basis in the complementarity of the sexes, a differentiation which is to be unified through marriage. Prior to examining Hegel's views on marriage, I will detail his position concerning the nature of this complementarity.

Hegel's tenets concerning woman's nature, although expressed through the terms and values of his philosophy, end up being remarkably similar to those of Rousseau. Woman is associated with the emotions, man with reason. Woman is passive, man, active. In Hegel's words,

One sex [man] is mind in its self-diremption into explicit personal self-subsistence and the knowledge and volition of free universality, i.e. the self-consciousness of conceptual thought and the volition of the objective final end. The other sex [woman] is mind maintaining itself in unity as knowledge and volition of the substantive, but knowledge and volition in the form of concrete individuality and feeling. In relation to externality, the former is powerful and active, the latter passive and subjective.[50]

Man's understanding is self-conscious and conceptual. He is aware of what he knows, and his knowledge is categorical in nature. Woman's understanding is intuitive and derives from her subjective feelings. Her understanding is implicit in her actions, but is not experienced at a conceptual level. Man is capable of comprehending objective, universal truths, while woman deals with the specifics of the subjective realm.

Hegel's conclusions concerning the consequences of these differences for the social roles of women and men are predictable. He claims that these differences dictate the exclusion of woman from the state. While man's life consists of learning, labor, and struggle within the public sphere of the state, woman is to focus on piety within the family.

In his *Encyclopaedia*, Hegel offers a physiological justification of these gender differences. Rather than woman's role in reproduction, Hegel points to the genitals to account for the differential abilities and capacities he attributes to the sexes. Hegel accepts the common scientific view that the male and female genitalia are homologous. He claims, for example, that the testicle corresponds to the female ovary and the prostate corresponds to the uterus. He argues, however, that the male genitalia are superior to the female, by insisting that the essential part of the female genitals "is necessarily the undifferentiated element, while in the male it is the sundered element of opposition."[51] In other words, although female and male genitals are homologous, the female genitals retain the more general or primitive structures, while the male genitals are the result of an evolution from this generic form and thus represent the differentiated element. Hegel, for example, explains that the testicles, while resembling the ovaries, possess additional structures not present in the ovary. Consistent with Hegel's metaphysic is the belief that the differentiated element represents the more evolved and thus more superior form. That the male genitalia are differentiated is then proof of the superiority of the male.

Hegel does not stop here, but rather posits a variety of correlations between the specific qualities of female and male genitals and mental abilities.* Identifying the ovary as corresponding to the testicle, and insisting that

---

* This inference is not idiosyncratic. It was a common tenet of nineteenth-century science to assume a correlation between the nature of one's genitals and mental capabilities. For a further discussion of such theories see my book *The Misbegotten Man*.

the testicle is differentiated while the ovary is not, Hegel concludes that since in the female the ovary "fails to emerge into opposition," it "does not become an independent and active cerebrality."[52] He tells us that the clitoris corresponds to inactive feeling, while its counterpart, the penis, corresponds to active sensibility. Additionally, Hegel equates the effusion of blood into the penis upon erection with menstrual discharges. With an imaginative but very traditional leap, Hegel concludes from this that "the simple retention of the conception in the uterus, is differentiated in the male into productive cerebrality and the external vital [the life-force]." The ultimate consequence of these differences is that "the male is the active principle; as the female remains in her undeveloped unity, she constitutes the principle of conception."[53]

Hegel thus believes that these physiological differences manifest themselves in terms of consciousness. Woman is capable of consciousness, but hers is less fully developed than that of man. Woman's inferior cerebrality results in her preclusion from the highest realms of reason. "They are not made for activities which demand a universal faculty such as the more advanced sciences, philosophy, and certain forms of artistic production. Women may have happy ideas, taste, and elegance, but they cannot attain to the ideal."[54] Men act on the basis of reason, women on the basis of feelings, inclinations, and opinions. Women "breathe in ideas," men acquire knowledge through the "stress of thought." The frequently quoted passage concerning woman's plant-like state, "The difference between men and women is like that between animals and plants," thus refers to woman's undifferentiated state.[55] Hegel did not mean that woman is incapable of ideas, but rather that she, like a plant, represents a less evolved, less developed state. But the conclusion is inescapable that her state is inferior to that of man.

It might be objected that my account is unfair to Hegel, for he, like Rousseau, saw the superior state not as that represented in the male, but in the unity of the male and the female. Through marriage, the sundered ethical substantiality manifest in woman and man, the immediacy of woman's ethical being and the dirempted, or split, mind of man who balances individual will and the universality of rational action, becomes a concrete unity. Marriage, "one of the absolute principles on which the ethical life of a community depends . . . results from the free surrender by both sexes of their personality" into the unity known as the family.[56] The union of female and male into the family constitutes the first ethical relation. "Marriage, and especially monogamy, is one of the absolute principles on which the ethical life of a community depends."[57] The family thus becomes the basis for all other relationships.

However, the family's existence is represented not only in relations between individuals but also through property. "The family, as person, has its real external existence in property; and it is only when this property takes the form of capital that it becomes the embodiment of the substantial personality of the family."[58] The family thus manifests a legal dimension, but the relationship of husband and wife to this resulting relation is not the same. Although both husband and wife are to surrender their personalities, it is the husband who maintains control of the resulting entity. "The family as a legal entity in relation to others must be represented by the husband as its head."[59] Even in the unity of the family, the male maintains the role of authority, for only he is capable of representing the legal concerns of the family within civil society, only he is capable of participation in the state. It appears, thus, that personalities are not fully surrendered. The distinction between woman as passive and feeling and man as active and conscious is maintained even in the family. Furthermore, since the acquisition and distribution of property is for Hegel a means to the realization of personal freedom, man's rule within the family further reinforces woman's passivity.[60]

But it is also important to realize that for Hegel, the family, although he characterizes it as constituting the root of ethical life, is the least evolved of all the realms. This fact becomes most clear in Hegel's discussion of the modern state. The realm of the family remains static, according to Hegel's account, unchanging from the pagan to the modern state. The public realm, on the other hand, undergoes an important evolution from the pagan to the modern state. Since man, being capable of higher consciousness, leaves the unity of the family and through participation in the state becomes actualized, we find important changes in the consciousness of man in the modern state. Woman, however, incapable of higher consciousness, must remain in the family, and thus like the family, her consciousness remains unaffected by the transition from the pagan to the modern state.

According to Hegel, the most important change from the pagan to the modern state is the evolution from the twofold division of human consciousness into the human law of the *polis* and the divine law of the family, to the three-part division of the family, civil society, and the state. In the modern world, the family represents the "ethical mind in its natural or immediate phase," civil society becomes the sphere in which particular interests are represented, that is, ethical life "in its division and appearance," and the state is the manifestation of the unification of the particular and the universal, "the end and actuality of both the substantial universal order and the public life devoted thereto."[61]

The family in the modern state, as in the pagan, is the foundation for the individual's earliest identification with the unity of a greater whole. The family is thus the initial source of the sentiment that allows for the movement from particular to universal. The individual relates to the family as a unity, considering not her or his individual interests or needs, but rather those of the family as a unit. Nevertheless, this identification is not with the universe of individuals, but only this small group. Additionally, the identification is immediate, rather than self-conscious and conceptual.

The modern world, according to Hegel, represents an evolution of the state from the *polis* to the mediation of civil society, "which intervenes between the family and the state" and "is the achievement of the modern world which has for the first time given all determinations of the [ethical] Idea their due."[62] Civil society, a sphere from which women are prohibited, allows for the expression of individual self-interest and thus the development of individuality. Through interaction in civil society, in particular through economic life and labor, men actualize themselves by realizing their arbitrary individual wills. "In this class-system, the ethical frame of mind therefore is rectitude and *esprit de corps*, i.e. the disposition to make oneself a member of one of the moments of civil society by one's own act, through one's energy, industry, and skill, to maintain oneself in this position, and to fend for oneself only through this process of mediating oneself with the universal, while in this way gaining recognition both in one's own eyes and in the eyes of others."[63] There is no recognition by Hegel that woman's role in the family involves labor and thus could provide a source for similarly developing her individual will.

The state is the moment of resolution of the particularity of civil society and the immediate universality of the family. The interdependence of men within the civil society gives rise to a consciousness of the commonality of interests. Thus what Hegel calls the "principle of subjectivity," the development of individuality which occurs in the state, gives rise to "substantive unity," the modern state in which "the universal [is] bound up with the complete freedom of its particular members and with private well-being."[64] That is, the modern state, unlike the *polis*, synthesizes the particular and the universal. It is only in the modern state that the individual citizen identifies with the objective order of the state. In the modern state, reason becomes, for the first time, fully conscious. The individual recognizes that his will and the objective order of the state are identical. Thus the law of the state is an expression of the will of the individual. The laws "are not something alien to the subject. On the contrary, his spirit bears witness to them as to its own essence, the essence in which he has a feeling of his selfhood, and in which he lives as in his own element which is not distinguished from himself. The subject is thus directly linked to the ethical order by a relation which is more like an identity than even the relation of faith or trust."[65] The state, according to Hegel, is the realm of rational freedom in which individual freedom is achieved only in conjunction with the freedom of all others.

The evolution from the *polis* to the modern state represents for Hegel a crucial evolution of the consciousness of man. Through the course of history, man has undergone the arduous and complex process of self-development. Modern man, in the words of Hegel, has experienced "self-diremption into explicit personal self-subsistence and the knowledge and volition of free universality, i.e. the self-consciousness of conceptual thought and the volition of the objective final end."[66] That is, the consciousness of modern man has transcended the Greek separation of particularity and universality and has experienced the highest form of rationality, the consciousness of the unity of particular and universal. Only the modern man has accomplished the full and actual development of individuality. Only the modern man is capable of achieving freedom.

And what of modern woman? In the words of Heidi Ravven, "The history of consciousness is exclusively the history of the male transcendence of Creon but the female perpetuation of Antigone."[67] Modern woman, limited by her very biology to the realm of the family, is incapable of the evolution of consciousness resulting from the development of individuality in civil society or the recognition of unity in the state. The modern woman, like the Greek woman, cannot escape the immediacy and unself-consciousness of the family. Unable to enter civil society, she cannot develop her individuality. Since it is through civil society that man comes to understand and participate fully in ethical life, only man fully participates in spirit. The family life precludes woman from developing full rationality or achieving true freedom.

Confined by nature to the realm of the family, women are incapable of the very evolution Hegel defines as the goal of the dialectic of spirit. Women, limited by the natural differences of their gender, impeded by their limited consciousness, are, it seems, outside the realm of the dialectic. Only men are capable of the actualization of spirit. Of course, Hegel limits this identification with spirit to men living in the modern bourgeois state, but nevertheless all men at least possess this potentiality. Even the evilest of men is, according to Hegel, moved by spirit. "If spiritual contingency or caprice goes forth into evil, that which goes astray is still infinitely superior to the regular movement of stars, or the innocent life of the plant, *because that which errs is still spirit*."[68] But a woman, no matter what ethical moment of the dialectical history of consciousness she participates in, is, like the innocent plant, precluded from the actualization of spirit. The movement of the dialectic into the modern state has thus left women behind.

Hegel's stance on woman is deeply in tension with his philosophical system.[69] According to Hegel, consciousness, that is, spirit, is of one kind. Hegel insists that even the spirit of God and of man are the same. "There cannot be two kinds of reason and two kinds of spirit . . . human reason, human spiritual consciousness or consciousness of its own essence, *is* reason generally, is the divine within humanity."[70] Woman's level of consciousness may be less developed than that of man; still it must be the same objective consciousness that participates in the dialectic, that is, shares the same universal logic. So how can Hegel declare that woman, by her very nature, is precluded from even the potential of actualization of spirit? The answer is that he cannot without contravening the very principles of his philosophy.

One of the core tenets of Hegel's philosophy is that spirit is preeminent over nature. "Nature is to be regarded as a *system of stages*, the one proceeding of necessity out of the other, and being the proximate truth of that from which it results. This is not to be thought of as a *natural* engendering of one out of the other however, but as an engendering within the inner Idea which constitutes the ground of nature."[71] According to Hegel, nature is transcended through the dialectical evolution. But when we look at Hegel's account of women's abilities, we find that it is nature rather than spirit that dictates their consciousness. In other words, a woman's very body pulls her out of the workings of spirit, thereby contravening Hegel's most basic tenet that spirit is the ultimate motivating force immanent in nature and history. According to Benjamin Barber, "Everywhere else dialectic triumphs, with women it is defeated by an obstinate nature that it can neither sublate, nor supersede, nor overcome. Nature may serve all other forms of consciousness as a transient vehicle for the actualization of spirit, but for women it is a quicksand bog from which there is no escape."[72]

Although Locke and Hegel differ radically with respect to the basic tenets upon which they ground their political theories, their positions concerning the role of women are surprisingly similar. Both theorists, despite their differences, argue that women are to be limited to the private realm of family, leaving the rule of the state as well as authority within the family in the hands of men. And both theorists ultimately base this conclusion upon the premise of the natural inferiority of women.

Locke's liberalist theory allows women a bit more agency than does Hegel's theory of the complementarity of the sexes. Locke, although accepting the premise of the natural inferiority of women, allows that this inferiority can be mitigated in the case of the exceptional woman. The conditions of a woman's birth or circumstances can provide the basis for negotiating a more favorable marriage contract, thus modifying the extent of her husband's authority over her, and in very exceptional situations may provide her the basis even for entrance into the public realm, as in the case of queens. But for Hegel, a woman's difference cannot be modified either by the specific circumstances of her birth or by the course of history. Hegel's woman is eternally limited to the realm of family.

Despite the fact that Locke allows the exceptional woman more freedom than does Hegel, the Hegelian system places more value on the position of women in the family than does the Lockean. Locke acknowledges the role women play in the rearing and education of their children but sees the private and public realms as basically separate and unrelated. Locke depicts the vast majority of women as functioning as caretakers of children and helpmeets to their husbands, but their activities are not viewed by him as directly contributing to the public realm of government. Hegel, in perceiving the realm of family and state in a relationship of dynamic interdependence, accords woman's role a value not found in the philosophy of Locke. Women, for Hegel, are the guardians of divine law, the law of the family. Although he clearly marks this law as inferior to that of man's human law, the two laws are interdependent, the one dependent on the other for its existence. Thus Hegel, contrary to Locke, does not see woman's role in the family as separate from man's role in the state. The two realms are interdependent and inseparable. So while Locke's liberalist theory offers to the exceptional woman more agency than is accorded to women by Hegel, the Hegelian system places a higher value on the role of women within the family than does the Lockean.

What is most interesting in the comparison of Locke and Hegel is that despite their vast theoretical differences, both implicate biology as the ultimate cause of woman's inferiority to man. Both Locke and Hegel can thus be seen as subscribing to the tenet I detailed in Chapter Two—the male is the true form. Both Hegel and Locke, like Plato and Aristotle before them, concur that woman is less capable of developing the "higher" faculties. Both attribute to her inferior rational capacities, Locke concluding from this that it must be the husband who retains authority over property within the family, Hegel insisting that woman is incapable of self-conscious knowledge of what is ethical. Furthermore, I have shown that for each of them, the force of this prejudice of woman's inferiority is so strong that they were willing to contravene their most basic doctrines, Locke being unable to recognize and apply the full force of his liberalist tenets, Hegel violating his most fundamental principle that spirit is preeminent over nature.

FURTHER READINGS

Primary Texts

LOCKE
Two Treatises of Government
First Treatise, chapters IV, V, VI
Second Treatise, chapters II, VI, VII, VIII, IX

HEGEL
Phenomenology of Spirit
VI.A.a, "The Ethical World"
VI.A.b, "Ethical Action"
Philosophy of Nature, section 368, "The Sex-Relationship"
Philosophy of Right, third part, especially "The Family"

Secondary Texts

LOCKE AND WOMAN/THE FEMININE
Butler, Melissa A. "Early Liberal Roots of Feminism: John Locke and the Attack on Patriarchy." *American Political Science Review* 72 (1978): 135–150.
Clark, Lorenne M. G. "Women and Locke: Who Owns the Apples in the Garden of Eden?" In *The Sexism of Social and Political Theory: Women and Reproduction from Plato to Nietzsche*. Ed. Lorenne M. G. Clark and Lynda Lange. Toronto: University of Toronto Press, 1979.
Coole, Diana H. *Women in Political Theory: From Ancient Misogyny to Contemporary Feminism*. Sussex: Wheatsheaf Books, 1988. Chapter 4.
Elshtain, Jean Bethke. *Public Man, Private Woman: Women in Social and Political Thought*. Princeton: Princeton University Press, 1981. Chapter 3.

HEGEL AND WOMAN/THE FEMININE
Benhabib, Seyla. "On Hegel, Women and Irony." In *Feminist Interpretations and Political Theory*. Ed. Mary Lyndon Shanley and Carole Pateman. University Park, PA: Pennsylvania State University Press, 1991.
Elshtain, Jean Bethke. *Public Man, Private Woman: Women in Social and Political Thought*. Princeton: Princeton University Press, 1981. Chapter 4.
Hodge, Joanna. "Women and the Hegelian State." In *Women in Western Political Philosophy: Kant to Nietzsche*. Ed. Ellen Kennedy and Susan Mendus. New York: St. Martin's Press, 1987.
Lloyd, Genevieve. *The Man of Reason: "Male" and "Female" in Western Philosophy*. Minneapolis: University of Minnesota Press, 1984. Chapters 4–6.
Mills, Patricia Jagentowicz. "Hegel and 'The Woman Question': Recognition and Intersubjectivity." In *The Sexism of Social and Political Theory: Women and Reproduction from Plato to Nietzsche*. Ed. Lorenne M. G. Clark and Lynda Lange. Toronto: University of Toronto Press, 1979.
———. *Woman, Nature, and Psyche*. New Haven: Yale University Press, 1987.

WOMEN AND POLITICAL THEORY

Brown, Wendy. *Manhood and Politics: A Feminist Reading in Political Theory*. Totowa, NJ: Rowman & Littlefield, 1988.

Clark, Lorenne M. G., and Lynda Lange, eds. *The Sexism of Social and Political Theory: Women and Reproduction from Plato to Nietzsche*. Toronto: University of Toronto Press, 1979.

Coole, Diana H. *Women in Political Theory: From Ancient Misogyny to Contemporary Feminism*. Sussex: Wheatsheaf Books, 1988.

Di Stefano, Christine. *Configurations of Masculinity: A Feminist Perspective on Modern Political Theory*. Ithaca: Cornell University Press, 1991.

Elshtain, Jean Bethke. *Public Man, Private Woman: Women in Social and Political Thought*. Princeton: Princeton University Press, 1981.

Evans, Judith, et al., eds. *Feminism and Political Theory*. London: Sage Publications, 1986.

Kennedy, Ellen, and Susan Mendus, eds. *Women in Western Political Philosophy: Kant to Nietzsche*. New York: St. Martin's Press, 1987.

Nicholson, Linda J. *Gender and History: The Limits of Social Theory in the Age of the Family*. New York: Columbia University Press, 1986.

Okin, Susan Moller. *Justice, Gender and the Family*. New York: Basic Books, 1989.

————. *Women in Western Political Thought*. Princeton: Princeton University Press, 1979.

Pateman, Carole. *The Sexual Contract*. Stanford: Stanford University Press, 1988.

Pateman, Carole and Elizabeth Gross, eds. *Feminist Challenges: Social and Political Theory*. Boston: Northeastern University Press, 1987.

Saxonhouse, Arlene W. *Women in the History of Political Thought: Ancient Greece to Machiavelli*. New York: Praeger, 1985.

Shanley, Mary Lyndon, and Carole Pateman, eds. *Feminist Interpretations and Political Theory*. University Park, PA: Pennsylvania State University Press, 1991.

WOMEN IN SEVENTEENTH-CENTURY ENGLAND AND NINETEENTH-CENTURY GERMANY

Ezell, Margaret J. M. *The Patriarch's Wife: Literary Evidence and the History of the Family*. Chapel Hill: University of North Carolina Press, 1987.

Fout, John C. *German Women in the Nineteenth Century: A Social History*. New York: Holmes & Meier, 1984.

Fraser, Antonia. *The Weaker Vessel: Woman's Lot in Seventeenth-Century England*. New York: Knopf, 1984.

Henderson, Katherine O., and Barbara F. McManus. *Half Humankind: Con-*

texts and Texts of the Controversy about Women in England, 1540–1640.
Urbana: University of Illinois Press, 1985.

Joeres, Ruth-Ellen B., and Mary Jo Maynes. *German Women in the Eighteenth and Nineteenth Centuries: A Social and Literary History.* Bloomington: Indiana University Press, 1986.

Prior, Mary, ed. *Women in English Society, 1500–1800.* New York: Methuen, 1985.

EPILOGUE:
THE CHALLENGE OF FEMINISM

In rejecting the gaze of the Elders and denying their definition of her as an adulterer, Susanna removed the scales from her own eyes. Her courage transformed her vision and she began to perceive that which before had remained hidden. She could now discern the gaze from outside the garden walls, the gaze that in defining her as "woman" rendered her inferior. She began to question all that she had been taught. Why was she, Susanna, defined only as wife of Joakim? Was her entire being and purpose to be contained in that one relationship? In asking this question Susanna realized that other women were defined differently. She saw that her maids were not defined as wife of Aaron or of Jacob. They were defined as maids of Susanna, wife of Joakim. She came to see that there were many ways in which the gaze from outside the garden walls defined women.

And Susanna found that she could not resist this gaze without also acknowledging how it defined men. She saw that the honor given to Joakim was based on his wealth, rather than the love and nurturance he gave to his children or to his wife. And she saw for the first time the men who were the slaves of Joakim, and she realized that they were men, yet were not perceived as fully human. She came to understand that honor and worth were defined in terms of qualities many people were prohibited from acquiring—wealth, education, political power—while other qualities which Susanna embraced as virtues—empathy, nurturance, patience—were virtually ignored.

And Susanna realized that there were many changes to be made.

❧

Reading as a woman we discover that there are indeed many changes to be made. Such a strategy of reading illustrates the falsity of the supposition that either readers or discourse is gender-neutral. We find woven throughout the philosophical canon a system of gender assumptions. In the course of writing these chapters, I have endeavored to highlight the patterns of these beliefs. I have argued that philosophers from diverse time periods, writing from competing philosophical traditions, perpetuate a strikingly similar conception of woman—as inferior to man, less capable of reason, less capable of moral agency, as functioning primarily within the private realm of family. My intention has not been simply to display the sexism of certain canonical philosophers, but rather to expose the fact that assumptions concerning gender differences are often a fundamental component of a philosophical system. Furthermore, I have argued that these assumptions are so intricately woven into the theoretical structure of a philosopher's thought that removing them requires far more than simple revisions of the system.

This conception of woman, along with the tenet that readers and texts can be (and should be) gender-neutral, arises out of a long and complex tradition of understanding the world in terms of dualisms, that is, in terms of pairs of traits which are seen as oppositional and in which one term of the polarity is privileged over the other. Aristotle, for example, tells us that the Pythagoreans accepted ten such principles: "limit and unlimited, odd and even, one and plurality, right and left, male and female, resting and moving, straight and curved, light and darkness, good and bad, square and oblong." (*Metaphysics* 986a 23–25.) Others have included mind and body, form and matter, reason and emotion, objectivity and subjectivity, public and private, culture and nature. The history of such dualisms is not static, nor is it always consistent, but throughout this changing history, gender remains a basic metaphysical category.

It is this latter point, that gender is a basic metaphysical category, that is highlighted by the strategy of reading philosophy as a woman. We not only become sensitive to the definitions of woman as inferior to man or her exclusion from the realm of the political, we also perceive the ways in which reason and morality have been defined as masculine. We become aware that the gender of the reader of the texts of philosophy is not irrelevant. It is a fact that enters into the context of our encounters with the texts of philosophy. If, as entreated by Descartes, I attempt to eradicate all the influences of my body, if I attempt to proceed as a disinterested reader, as a genderless, thinking being, I will be quickly stymied by the fact that the texts of philosophy too often contain the depiction of woman as incapable of the type of cognitive ability required to be a Cartesian reader. I, a woman, cannot ignore my body when I am told that the female body precludes or impedes my ability to be rational, to be moral, to participate within the realm of politics. Reading as a woman, being embodied readers, undermines the image of the reader, as well as the text, as genderless.

An understanding of the gender assumptions underpinning philosophy provides the reader with a place, a standpoint, although a continually shifting one, from which to read such gendered structures. We cannot stand "outside the texts" to critique them, but we can use this understanding of the language of gender to move through the texts differently than we did in the past. The value of embodied reading is well expressed by Carol H. Cantrell in her essay "Analogy as Destiny: Cartesian Man and the Woman Reader":

> For a woman reader, the presence of a language of dualisms within the texts she reads means that she is represented in those texts at critical moments of suppression and valuation. Paradoxically, this language, which has in so many destructive ways shaped her experience and her sense of herself, can be turned inside out, so to speak, and used to track what has been denigrated and what has been lost. Though she cannot jump out of her culture's discourses or her own skin any more than the "man of reason" can, she can use her understanding of the language of gender as a lever to move her self into a new relationship to that language.[1]

This alternative approach to the texts of philosophy provides a basis for resisting the definitions of woman (and of man) and for acknowledging and recovering those experiences and abilities that have previously been denigrated because of their association with the feminine.

One of the first steps in turning the philosophy of dualisms "inside out" is to give voice to that which remains silent and unspoken. Luce Irigaray in her book *The Speculum of the Other Woman* offers a model of this approach to reading.[2] Sensitive to the movements of gender in the texts of Descartes, Freud, Hegel, Kant, Lacan, and Plato, Irigaray carefully delineates the systematic exclusion of the feminine in their theories. For example, in her essay "Plato's *Hystera*," Irigaray offers a very different reading of the Platonic cave metaphor of the ascent to wisdom. She carefully discloses the ways in which Plato's discourse was constructed as a masculine discourse between men. Demonstrating in this way the systematic exclusion of the feminine from the myth of the cave, Irigaray argues that far from being absent, the feminine actually plays a vital function in the masculine economy of the cave by providing the silent matrix which reflects the masculine—what Irigaray calls "the memoryless mirror of representation."[3] Thus, the task of the woman reader, according to Irigaray, is to subvert the dualisms of masculine discourse by unveiling the feminine which has been concealed by the discourse of men.[4] According to Andrea Nye, Irigaray's method "clears the way for a new kind of feminist thinking. Once the simple presence/absence of phallic logic is abandoned, the feminine can appear as a value in its own right opening the way . . . for a real, not sham, sexual difference in which both sexes are valorized."[5]

In adopting such a strategy, indeed in accepting my challenge to read philosophy as a woman, it is tempting to simply reverse the valorization of traits identified as masculine and privilege those seen as feminine. But simply reversing the dualism only perpetuates it. If, for example, a feminist attempts to develop a theory of rationality that privileges the emotional over the rational, her or his "success" in such an endeavor is suspect. It is doubtful that a theorist could in fact achieve an empowerment of the feminine using the very dichotomy which defines the female as inferior. As long as the rationality of male thought remains the standard by which feminine virtues are judged, they will always be found wanting. To subvert the standard itself requires undermining the very dualisms simple reversal perpetuates. The focus on the dualisms thus must aim at dislocating the boundaries between the polarities.

Reading as a woman makes us aware of the hidden fact of the androcentrism of the traditional discourses of philosophy. But as we become aware of the presuppositions of masculine discourse in the texts of the philosophers, we in turn become aware of the ways in which gender assumptions are inextricably intertwined with others such as race, class, and sexuality. Our location as a reader is neither fixed nor unitary, but rather multiple and dispersed. In our focus on gender we cannot neglect the other sites of polarization—white/nonwhite, rich/poor, heterosexual/homosexual—for the exchange among these various divisions is continual.

My analysis in this book makes clear the depth of the challenge feminism poses for philosophy. A canonical philosopher's views about women cannot simply be dismissed as not being integral to his central philosophical doctrines. Philosophers' gender assumptions often affect the central categories of their system—their conceptions of rationality, their construals of the nature of morality, their visions of the public realm. Feminist critiques thus pose a serious challenge to mainstream Western philosophy, requiring a careful reevaluation of its basic concepts.

Feminist critiques like that contained within this book unveil the severity of the problems posed to women by the central categories of Western philosophy. We cannot, for example, expect that all people will be seen as equally rational when the philosophical definitions of rationality privilege traits viewed as masculine. Feminist theorists have argued that Western conceptions of objectivity and the corresponding separation of knower from the known are a part of this emphasis of masculine traits.[6] A gender-neutral conception of rationality will thus require changes throughout the philosophical system.

One central concern of feminist critiques of rationality is to question the denigration of the emotions and the perception of the body as an impediment to knowledge. Seeing knowledge as grounded in experience, theorists such as Nancy Hartsock, Sara Ruddick, and Hilary Rose argue that the activities assigned to women, understood through the categories of feminist theory, provide a starting point for developing claims to knowledge that are potentially more comprehensive and less distorted than those of privileged men.[7] They believe that women's sensuous, relational, and contextual perspective allows them to understand aspects of nature and social life not available to those men who are cut off from such activities. Thus women's experiences provide a basis for developing an alternative epistemology that unifies manual, mental, and emotional activity. For example, Sara Ruddick develops a theory of what she calls "maternal thinking." Ruddick argues that the "agents of maternal practice, acting in response to the demands of their children, acquire a conceptual scheme—a vocabulary and logic of connections—through which they order and express the facts and values of their practice. In judgments and self-reflection, they refine and concretize this scheme. Intellectual activities are distinguishable but not separable from disciplines of feeling. There is a unity of reflection, judgment, and emotion."[8] Similarly, Patricia Hill Collins sketches an alternative epistemology based on the standpoint of black women's experiences. Collins discusses two features of this standpoint.

First, Black women's political and economic status provides them with a distinctive set of experiences that offers a different view of material reality than that available to other groups. The unpaid and paid work that Black women perform, the types of communities in which they live, and the kinds of relationships they have with others suggest that African-American women, as a group, experience a different world than those who are not Black and not female. Second, these experiences stimulate a distinctive Black female consciousness concerning that material reality.[9]

Collins argues that in articulating this standpoint, Black women often employ an alternative epistemology that reflects these experiences as well as embracing Afrocentric values. Collins delineates four central features of this epistemology: concrete experience as a criterion of meaning; the use of dialogue in assessing knowledge claims; the ethic of caring; and the ethic of personal accountability.[10]

Many of the alternative epistemologies developed by feminists attempt to develop a conception of rationality that involves a "unity" of emotion and reason. But the lesson learned from careful attention to the history of philosophy is that this blending cannot be simply additive, but must be transformative. As can be seen from my analysis of Rousseau, it is not sufficient for feminists simply to attempt to construct a theory of rationality that includes both masculine and feminine traits. As long as masculine traits are ranked as superior to feminine traits, such theories would modify but not correct the gender bias. Feminists must carefully undercut the subtle ranking of masculine over feminine traits.

Part of the process of questioning this ranking has involved critiques of dualistic thought. Feminists have argued that all knowledge involves values and politics. Feminist science criticism, for example, is aimed at demonstrating the ways in which factors such as the social and political identity of a scientist, including her or his gender experiences, are part of the practice of science.[11] This dissolution of the boundary between science and values or politics has in turn opened the way to a revised conception of the knowing subject. Rather than the disinterested, disembodied Cartesian knower, feminists are offering a conception of the knowing subject as situated, as engaged, and as a part of a community. For example, Lynn Harkinson Nelson has argued that "who knows" is not individuals, but communities. Accepting the view of theorists such as Hartsock, Rose, and Ruddick that our experiences as women are epistemologically significant, Nelson reminds us of the necessity of interpersonal relationships and of a public conceptual scheme for knowing. Nelson argues that our experiences of the world arise out of a conceptual scheme, a system of theories about the world that we inherit when we learn to speak and act within society, and which we continue to learn and refine throughout our lives. Nelson concludes that "what constitutes evidence for a claim is not determined by individuals, but by the standards a community accepts concomitantly with constructing, adopting, and refining theories. Those standards constrain what it is possible for an individual to believe as well as the theorizing we engage in together."[12] Feminist critiques of dualistic thinking offer radically transformed notions of the basic epistemological categories, including objectivity, the knowing subjects, and truth.

Feminists are working on similar transformations of moral theories. The critiques parallel those of rationality. Feminists argue that the basic categories of moral theory lead to a definition of moral competence as masculine; that is, the moral agent is perceived as male. Thus traditional ethical theory is seen as insufficient to address the concerns and experiences of women. Rather than attempt to argue that women are capable of full moral agency as traditionally defined, feminist ethicists are working to reconstruct moral theory. Traditional moral theory is criticized for positing a conception of people as disinterested, independent individuals, who are both free and equals, and of a moral agent as impartial.[13] Many feminist theorists argue instead for a model of moral thinking based on relationships, with moral actions arising out of responsibilities and affiliations rather than duties or rights.

Currently the most influential of these alternative models of morality is what has been labeled an "ethics of care." Advanced in large part by the work of Carol Gilligan, Nel Noddings, and Sara Ruddick, an ethics of care replaces the autonomous moral agent who uses reason to understand and apply a set of universal moral rules with the member of a community who responds to others in a caring way that aims to prevent harm and to sustain relationships.[14] Many of the care theorists believe that the experience of rearing a child provides the basis of an alternative moral sensibility, and that the mother-child relationship can provide a new model for moral relationships.[15] It is believed that such transformations of ethical theory will both acknowledge the experiences of women and include issues of special concern to women, both of which are neglected in traditional ethical theory.

As with feminist research in epistemology, current work in feminist ethics is both exciting and promising. Still, it is important that we keep the lessons of history clearly before us. Feminists have identified the ways in which women are excluded from moral agency when morality is defined in terms of traits perceived as masculine. As I noted in my discussion of Kant, when the characteristics used to define the moral individual are seen as masculine, a woman must overcome or control her feminine qualities and become like a man in order to act morally. This will lead to the belief that it is more difficult for a woman to be moral than for a man. But it is easier to miss the ways in which a moral theory that includes attributes perceived as feminine in addition to those accepted as masculine can nevertheless exclude women.

What we learn from a careful study of Hume's moral theory is, first of all, that it is not sufficient to simply infuse traditional moral theory with traits seen as feminine. As mentioned before, it will not be sufficient to simply "mix in" qualities viewed as feminine. Those traits perceived as masculine are ranked higher and seen as more valuable than those accepted as feminine. Thus to simply add in so-called "feminine components" will not erase such ranking. Feminists who are concerned to correct the omission of the "feminine" must also develop a moral theory which rejects the ways in which masculine traits are privileged over feminine traits. Some theorists believe that this can be accomplished while retaining the distinction between feminine and masculine; others believe that the distinction itself will have to be eradicated. I believe it is premature to come to a conclusion concerning this debate. The distinction between feminine and masculine and its various theoretical permutations must be examined carefully and critically in order to determine whether it should be retained, revised, or rejected.

A second lesson that we learn from Hume is that moral theory does not exist in a vacuum. Despite the potential gender neutrality of Hume's moral theory, his acceptance of an Aristotelian view of woman's natural inferiority led him to conclude that women would be less likely to act morally than men. So even if feminists are successful in advancing and finding acceptance for a moral theory that does not privilege masculine traits, as long as socially held beliefs about women's inferiority persist, we must not think that such a moral theory will be sufficient to eradicate the perception that woman is less capable of moral action than man. We cannot limit our critiques simply to moral theory or to theories of rationality. We must also transform the gaze from outside the garden walls that defines woman as inferior. Feminist theorists must never forget that our political action goes hand in hand with our theorizing.

In addition, in developing theories which include or are modeled on women's experiences and which address issues, whether in ethics or in science, associated with women that had been previously neglected, it is important to explicitly undermine the assumption that such experiences are limited to women or that women's concern for such issues is innate or inevitable. Given the gender essentialism that persists in contemporary scientific, religious, and commonsense views, such theories run the risk of reinforcing such stereotypes unless the theory is carefully and consciously designed to subvert them. One important component of this transformation is to recognize that the experiences and concerns of women, like those of men, are plural and diverse.[16]

Feminist criticisms of the public/private dichotomy are similarly complex. In identifying the ways in which various political theorists have excluded women or limited their participation in the state, one comes to the realization that this exclusion is not easily rectified. First of all, one must counter the persistent and powerful prejudice of woman's inferiority. As I have shown, theorists as diverse as Hegel and Locke were moved by the force of this prejudice to conclude that women are to be limited to the private realm of family. Second, as with theories of rationality and morality, feminist investigations of androcentric biases in political theory are showing that the political realm is constructed as masculine. The institutions of the political realm are, in the words of Wendy Brown, "saturated with highly problematic, often dangerous, ideals and practices of manhood."[17] Concepts such as freedom, political power, and property are defined in terms of masculinity.

As feminist critiques of versions of liberal feminism make clear, discrimination on the basis of gender will not be eradicated by simply attempting to include women within the public realm. As long as the values and activities of the private realm continue to be denigrated and as long as the prejudice of woman's inferiority goes unquestioned, so-called "equal opportunity" will be neither. Nor can we simply reverse the values and attempt to inscribe politics with "female virtues." Some of the characteristics that feminists offer as female virtues, such as a sense of community and empathy, are important and should be taken seriously in attempting to reconstruct society. But in recognizing that the feminine, as well as the masculine, is socially constructed, and in fact often constructed in reaction to the masculine, we have every reason to think that it too will be far too limited to universalize as characteristic of humanity. In the process of developing alternative political theories, feminists may decide to embrace traits constructed as feminine, but we must do so carefully. First of all, even the most positive of the so-called "female virtues," such as caring, are traditionally envisioned as involving negative aspects such as a failure to acknowledge one's own needs, being overprotective, and a fear of autonomy. As Wendy Brown cautions, the fact that

we like some of the sensibilities women have developed pursuant to the role they have been assigned historically is a good reason to explore the political potential of these sensibilities but does not mean we can develop them into an idealized and mobile value *system* that abstracts from the context in which the sensibilities were formed and eschews their less lovely aspects. Similarly, while the traditional work of women as mothers and managers of emotional life provides rich material for rethinking political relations, this experience cannot simply replace political relations.[18]

Second, in investigating the feminine it is crucial that differences between women arising from differences such as race, class, and culture not be erased. As Elizabeth Spelman reminds us, the concept of womanhood is not the same for all women and thus we cannot conclude that the sexism that all women experience is the same. "We have to understand what one's oppression 'as a woman' means in each case. The sexism most Black women have experienced has not typically included being put on a pedestal. Moreover, we cannot describe what it is to be subject to several forms of oppression, say, sexism and racism and classism, by adding together their separate accounts. For example, we surely cannot produce an accurate picture of Latina women's lives simply by combining an account of Anglo women's lives and one of Latino men's lives."[19]

The feminist challenge to philosophy is onerous. It goes far beyond the definitions of womanhood contained within specific philosophical accounts to reveal and question the gender bias woven into the concepts central to philosophy. I have discussed three of these—rationality, morality, and political agency—revealing the complexities of the impact of gender assumptions upon the construction and definition of these concepts. But my account only brushes the surface of the ways in which gender assumptions are woven into the fabric of philosophy. There are many more concepts needing similar analysis; there are patterns of bias not revealed in my account. Although I have provided a method for reading philosophy and identified a series of common assumptions, there is much more to be done. My challenge to you is to take the tools I have offered you, refine them, and use them to reread the entirety of the philosophical canon—this time with a focus on gender.

In this endeavor we must work together, for there are many changes to be made.

NOTES

Chapter One
1. *The Aprocrypha of the Old Testament* (New York: Thomas Nelson and Sons, 1957), Susanna, pp. 22–23.
2. Susanna, p. 43.
3. Susanna, p. 63.
4. See for example Richard H. Popkin, "The Philosophical Bases of Modern Racism," in *Philosophy and the Civilizing Arts*, ed. Craig Walton and John P. Anton (Athens: Ohio University Press, 1974).
5. Far more work needs to be done in these areas. However, some excellent discussions of the importance of race and the methods of race exclusion can be found in the following: two anthologies edited by Henry Louis Gates, Jr., *Black Literature & Literary Theory* (New York: Methuen, 1984), *"Race," Writing, and Difference* (Chicago: University of Chicago Press, 1986); *Black Women in America: Social Science Perspectives* edited by Micheline R. Malson, Elisabeth Mudimbe-Boyi, Jean F. O'Barr, and Mary Wyer; Patricia Hill Collins *Black Feminist Thought.* (Winchester, MA: Unwin Hyman, 1990), and Angela Y. Davis, *Women, Race and Class* (New York: Random House, 1981). For a discussion of the impact of race and ethnicity upon the concepts and problems of philosophy, I look forward to Lucius Outlaw's *Philosophy and Ethnicity*, a forthcoming volume in this Paragon Issues in Philosophy Series.
6. Jean-Jacques Rousseau, *Emile, or On Education*, trans. Allen Bloom (New York: Basic Books, 1979), book V, p. 387.
7. See, for example, the essays in Carol MacCormack and Marilyn Strathern, eds., *Nature, Culture and Gender* (London: Cambridge University Press, 1980).
8. Because of this decision, I will not compare these philosophers' views of woman and the feminine to those of women who developed philosophies during similar time periods. But such a study would be very interesting. For those interested in pursuing such an inquiry, the three-volume *A History of Women Philosophers* edited by Mary Ellen Waithe (Dordrecht: Kluwer Academic Publishers) is an excellent resource.
9. For a critical discussion of the controversy over this, see my article (coauthored with William Cowling) "Plato and Feminism." *APA Newsletter on Feminism and Philosophy* 90, 1 (1990): 110–115.
10. Many of the themes and ideas I touch upon in my Epilogue are developed in

detail in Eve Browning Cole's *Philosophy and Feminist Criticism*, a forthcoming volume in the Paragon Issues in Philosophy Series.

Chapter Two

1. For a detailed discussion of this claim see my forthcoming book, *The Misbegotten Man: Scientific, Religious, and Philosophical Conceptions of Woman's Nature* (Indiana University Press).

2. Hesiod, *Theogony, Works and Days, Shield*, trans. Apostolos Athanassakis (Baltimore: Johns Hopkins University Press, 1983), pp. 600–601.

3. For a recent example, see Gregory Vlastos, "Was Plato a Feminist?" *The Times Literary Supplement*, March 17–23, 1989. An overview of the controversy as to whether Plato's views about women are consistent with feminist principles can be found in my "Plato and Feminism" (with W. Cowling), *APA Newsletter on Feminism and Philosophy* 90, 1 (1990): 110–115.

4. For an important analysis of the problems resulting from treating women as a group, without reference to class or race differences, when analyzing Plato's views on women, see Elizabeth Spelman's *Inessential Woman* (Boston: Beacon Press, 1988).

5. For an interesting discussion of Plato's politicization of woman's body see Monique Canto, "The Politics of Women's Bodies: Reflections on Plato," in *The Female Body in Western Culture*, ed. Susan Rubin Suleiman (Cambridge: Harvard University Press, 1986).

6. Greater capacities for nurturing children and caring for the sick were seen by Xenophon in his *Oeconomicus* as feminine traits which the gods had given women. Trans. C. Lord (Ithaca: Cornell University Press, 1970).

7. As Spelman points out in her discussion of Plato in *Inessential Woman*, the distinction is actually not this sharp, for Plato did at times indicate that certain types of souls corresponded to, or ought to correspond to, a certain type of body, as, for example, when he argued in the *Laws* that a cowardly soul should be in a woman's body (944c). Still, Plato's dominant position is that significant differences between people are due to differences in their souls.

8. For a detailed discussion of the flaws of Aristotle's arguments in support of the equation of male seminal fluids and menses, see my "The Weaker Seed: The Sexist Bias of Reproductive Theory," in *Feminism and Science*, ed. Nancy Tuana (Bloomington: Indiana University Press, 1989).

9. Maryanne Clien Horowitz, in her article "Aristotle and Woman," *Journal of the History of Biology* 9 (1976): 183–213, suggests that Aristotle's view of women as monstrosities may have tied in with euthanasia practices in which defective children were often left in the open to die and rates of female infants so treated were much higher than male.

10. For a full discussion of Aristotle's biological investigations see Ingemar Düring, "Aristotle's Method in Biology," *Aristote et les problèmes de methode*, Symposium Aristoteticum, Louvain, Belgium, 1960. (Louvain: Centre de Wulf-Mansion, 1980, pp. 213–221) and Michael Boylan, *Method and Practice in Aristotle's Biology* (Lanham, MD: University Press of America, 1983).

11. For a discussion of slavery in ancient Greece, see M. I. Finley, *Ancient Slavery and Modern Ideology*. Hammondsworth: Penguin, 1983. For a detailed comparison of Aristotle's views of slave and free women, see Spelman's *Inessential Woman*, Chapter 2.

Chapter Three
1. For an excellent development of this theme of appropriation, see Page duBois, *Sowing the Body: Psychoanalysis and Ancient Representations of Women* (Chicago: University of Chicago Press, 1988).
2. My discussion here will be limited to Western conceptions of reason and rationality. For further discussion of this question see Susan Bordo, *The Flight to Objectivity: Essays on Cartesianism and Culture* (Albany: State University of New York Press, 1987); Sandra Harding, *The Science Question in Feminism* (Ithaca: Cornell University Press, 1986); Susan Hekman, *Gender and Knowledge: Elements of a Postmodern Feminism* (Boston: Northeastern University Press, 1990); Evelyn Fox Keller, *Reflections on Gender and Science* (New Haven: Yale University Press, 1985); and Genevieve Lloyd, *The Man of Reason: "Male" and "Female" in Western Philosophy*. (Minneapolis: University of Minnesota, 1984.)
3. Jean Grimshaw in *Philosophy and Feminist Thinking* (Minneapolis: University of Minnesota Press, 1986) criticizes the attempt to argue for the maleness of philosophy or, in the case of Descartes, reason, on the ground that conceptions of femininity and masculinity are complex and shifting. Although I agree with her claim that the terms are cluster concepts—that is, a list of characteristics loosely associated and such that the constitutive traits shift over time and place—still there has been a strong core association within Western thought that associates man with activity and reason and woman with passivity and emotion. See, for example, Lloyd, *The Man of Reason*; Robin M. Shott, *Cognition and Eros: A Critique of the Kantian Paradigm* (Boston: Beacon Press, 1988); and my *The Misbegotten Man*.
4. An additional question being asked by feminists who are examining the question of the maleness of reason is whether Western conceptions of reason and rationality are the result of distinctively masculine experiences and interests. Bordo, for example, in *The Flight to Objectivity*, argues that the Cartesian rejection of the feminine is a consequence of the anxiety men experience as a result of their separation from the maternal, which Bordo defines as the immanent realms of earth, nature, and the authority of the body.
5. *History of Animals* 608b 10–12.
6. Descartes, *Rules for the Direction of the Mind*, in *The Philosophical Works of Descartes*, trans. E. Haldane and G. Ross (New York: Dover, 1955), rule VII, p. 19.
7. Ibid., rule XII, p. 46.
8. Ibid., p. 47.
9. Ibid., rule IV, p. 9.
10. Ibid., rule III, p. 7.
11. Descartes, *Meditations on First Philosophy*, in *The Philosophical Works of Descartes*, trans. E. Haldane and G. Ross (New York: Dover, 1955), meditation III, p. 157.
12. For an extended discussion of this point see Stanley Rosen, *Plato's* Symposium (New Haven: Yale University Press, 1968).
13. Descartes, *Passions of the Soul*, in *The Philosophical Works of Descartes*, trans. E. Haldane and G. Ross (New York: Dover, 1955), article XLVII, p. 353.
14. Ibid., article XXVII, p. 344.
15. Ibid., article XXXIV, p. 347.
16. Descartes, *Meditations on First Philosophy*, meditation VI, p. 193.
17. Descartes, *Passions of the Soul*, article L, p. 356.

18. Descartes, *Discourse on the Method of Rightly Conducting the Reason*, in *The Philosophical Works of Descartes*, trans. E. Haldane and G. Ross (New York: Dover, 1955), part I, p. 81.
19. Descartes, letter to Vatier, February 22, 1638, cited in Lloyd, *The Man of Reason*. As Lloyd points out, his insistence here was due in large part to his attempt to reject scholastic training as necessary to the acquisition of truth, and to replace it with individual reasoning.
20. Philo, *Questions and Answers on Exodus*, trans. Ralph Marcus (Cambridge: Harvard University Press, 1953), book 1, Question 8, pp. 15–16. Lloyd's *The Man of Reason* contains an excellent discussion of Philo's equation of reason and maleness.
21. Aquinas, *Summa Theologica*, Trans. Fathers of the English Dominican Province (Westminister, MD: Christian Classics, 1981), II.II.156.1.
22. Jacob Sprenger and Henry Kramer, *Malleus Maleficarium*, trans. Rev. Montague Summers (London: Pushkin Press, 1948), Part I, Question 6, p. 47.
23. Princess Elizabeth to Descartes, June 10–20, 1643, cited in Lloyd, *The Man of Reason*, pp. 48–49.
24. Aristotle, *Economics* 1343b 29–1344a 1.
25. Lest one think that our contemporary attitudes toward reason have shifted significantly since the seventeenth century, consider the following: "Mass education has altered male-female relations for good, by helping to bring women into the *wider world of male outlook and concerns*." Christopher Winch, "Women, Reason, and Education," *Journal of Philosophy of Education* 19, 1 (1985): 91–98, my emphasis.
26. For an excellent refutation of just this position, see Sara Ruddick, *Maternal Thinking: Toward a Politics of Peace* (Boston: Beacon, 1989).
27. Rousseau, "A Discourse on the Arts and Sciences," in *The Social Contract and Discourses*, trans. G. D. H. Cole (London: Dent, 1973), p. 26.
28. Rousseau, *Emile, or On Education*, trans. Allan Bloom (New York: Basic Books, 1979), book IV, p. 253.
29. For an excellent discussion of Rousseau's views concerning the relation of women to *amour de soi* and *amour propre*, a form of self-love Rousseau viewed as inferior, see Genevieve Lloyd, "Rousseau on Reason, Nature and Women," *Metaphilosophy*, 14, 3 and 4 (1983): 308–326.
30. Rousseau, *Emile*, book IV, pp. 212–213.
31. Rousseau, "A Discourse on the Origin of Inequality," in *The Social Contract and Discourses*, trans. G. D. H. Cole (London: Dent, 1973), p. 66.
32. Rousseau, *Emile*, book V, p. 358.
33. Ibid.
34. Ibid.
35. Ibid., pp. 358, 368, 370, 371.
36. Ibid., p. 365.
37. Ibid., p. 361.
38. Rousseau, "A Discourse on the Origin of Inequality," p. 230.
39. Ibid., p. 214.
40. Ibid., p. 239.
41. Rousseau, *Emile*, book V, p. 363.
42. Ibid., p. 365.
43. Emile is also educated in such a way as to inculcate certain traits, that is, characteristics Rousseau saw as fitting his role. It would be a mistake to think that

Rousseau's model of education is of a different type for Emile than for Sophie. Both are being formed by their teacher. For an excellent discussion of this point see Jane Roland Martin, *Reclaiming a Conversation: The Ideal of the Educated Woman* (New Haven: Yale University Press, 1985).

44. Rousseau, *Emile*, book V, p. 479.
45. Ibid.
46. Ibid., p. 478.
47. Ibid., book IV, p. 314, my emphasis.
48. Ibid., book V. p. 426.
49. Ibid., p. 386.
50. Rousseau attacked "intellectuals" who spend their time "on the brink of that well at the bottom of which Truth lies hid," instead of directing their energies to living well and pursuing a just society. However, he did not criticize all intellectuals, separating out those who can "walk alone in the footsteps" of Bacon, Descartes, or Newton, whom he labels "the teachers of mankind." These thinkers, unlike the bogus intellectuals, will "raise monuments to the glory of human understanding." ("A Discourse on the Arts and Sciences," part 2, pp. 159, 172–173.) It is thus a mistake to characterize Rousseau's position as one in which woman's practical reason is superior to man's theoretical reason, as Joel Schwartz in *The Sexual Politics of Jean-Jacques Rousseau* (Chicago: University of Chicago Press, 1984) comes dangerously close to doing. (See footnote 19 on that work's p. 168.)
51. Rousseau, *Emile*, book V, p. 359.
52. Rousseau, *The Social Contract*, trans. G. D. H. Cole (New York: Dutton, 1950), p. 56.
53. Ibid.
54. Rousseau, *Emile*, book IV, p. 211.
55. Rousseau, "Discourse on the Origin of Inequality," p. 229.
56. Rousseau, *Emile*, book V, p. 387.
57. Ibid.
58. Ibid., p. 376.
59. Ibid., p. 364. Furthermore, it appears possible for the exceptional man to transcend this dependence altogether. Rousseau, contrasting himself with Emile, viewed himself as a natural man who lived in a "savage state" independent of woman and of society. For a discussion of this point see Chapter 4 of Schwartz's *The Sexual Politics of Jean-Jacques Rousseau*.
60. Rousseau, *Emile*, Book V, p. 358.
61. Ibid., p. 445.
62. Ibid., p. 390.
63. Ibid., p. 636.
64. Ibid., p. 479.
65. For a detailed discussion of this point see Coole's chapter on Rousseau in *Women in Political Theory*.
66. For a developed discussion of this point see Lynda Lange's "Rousseau: Women and the General Will," in *The Sexism of Social and Political Theory: Women and Reproduction from Plato to Nietzsche*, ed. Lorenne M. G. Clark and Lynda Lange (Toronto: University of Toronto Press, 1979).

Chapter Four
1. An affirmative answer to this question has been developed by Carol Gilligan in her *In a Different Voice: Psychological Theory and Women's Development* (Cam-

bridge: Harvard University Press, 1982). Gilligan argues that a care perspective is prevalent in women's moral thinking while men often focus on a justice perspective when dealing with moral issues. For an overview of how this approach has been received by feminist theorists, see Eva Feder Kittay and Diana T. Meyers, eds., *Woman and Moral Theory* (Savage, MD: Rowman and Littlefield, 1987).

2. Kant, *Grounding for the Metaphysics of Morals*, trans. James W. Ellington (Indianapolis: Hackett, 1981), p. 11 (398).
3. Ibid., p. 35 (428).
4. Ibid.
5. Ibid., p. 13 (400).
6. Ibid., p. 14 (402).
7. Robin Schott in *Cognition and Eros: A Critique of the Kantian Paradigm* (Boston: Beacon Press, 1988) argues that Kant's discussion of objective knowledge in his *Critique of Pure Reason*, as well as in his moral theory, presents a description of human activity that parallels the phenomenon of fetishism later described by Marx in *Capital*.
8. Kant, *Grounding*, p. 23 (412).
9. Ibid., p. 34 (426).
10. Kant, *The Metaphysical Principles of Virtue*, trans. James Ellington (Indianapolis: Bobbs-Merrill, 1964), p. 48 (390).
11. Kant, *The Metaphysical Principles of Virtue*, p. 50 (392).
12. Kant, *Grounding*, p. 35 (428).
13. Kant, *Grounding*, p. 36 (429).
14. For a more complete development of this argument see Christine M. Korsgaard, "Kant's Formula of Humanity," *Kantstudien* 77 (1986): 183–202.
15. Kant, *The Metaphysical Principles of Virtue*, p. 84 (423).
16. Ibid., p. 51 (392).
17. Kant, *Grounding*, p. 41 (436).
18. Ibid., p. 48 (444).
19. "Introduction to the Theory of Right," in Kant, *Metaphysic of Morals*, in *Kant's Political Writings*, ed. Hans Reiss, trans. H. B. Nisbet (London: Cambridge University Press, 1971), p. 139.
20. Kant, *Observations on the Feeling of the Beautiful and Sublime*, trans. John Goldthwait (Berkeley: University of California Press, 1960), pp. 76–77.
21. Ibid., p. 77.
22. Ibid.
23. Kant, *Anthropology from a Pragmatic Point of View*. trans. Mary J. Gregor. The Hague, Netherlands: Martinus Nijhoff, 1974, p. 167 (303).
24. Kant, *The Metaphysical Principles of Virtue*, pp. 58–59 (400).
25. Kant, *Observations*, p. 78.
26. Ibid., p. 81.
27. Kant, *Anthropology*, p. 174 (312).
28. Kant, *Observations*, p. 111.
29. Ibid., p. 80.
30. Ibid., p. 79.
31. Kant, *Anthropology*, p. 169 (306).
32. Ibid.
33. Kant, *Observations*, p. 78.
34. Ibid., pp. 77–78, 81.

35. Kant, *Anthropology*, p. 171 (307–308).
36. Kant, *Observations*, p. 79.
37. In *The Educational Theory of Immanuel Kant*, trans. Edward F. Buckner (Philadelphia: J. B. Lippincott, 1904), p. 222, cited in Jean P. Rumsey, "The Development of Character in Kantian Moral Theory," *Journal of the History of Philosophy* XXVII, 2 (1989): 256.
38. Kant, *Observations*, p. 78.
39. Ibid., p. 86.
40. Ibid., p. 93.
41. Kant, *Anthropology*, p. 167 (303).
42. Jane Kneller in "Kant's Immature Imagination" in *Critical Feminist Essays in the History of Western Philosophy*, ed. Bat Ami Bar-On (State University of New York Press, forthcoming), offers an interesting discussion of the parallel in Kant's philosophy between the civilized woman and civilized imagination (taste), arguing that Kant viewed each as functioning to cultivate and refine society yet believed that neither necessarily led to morality.
43. Kant, *The Metaphysical Principles of Virtue*, p. 108 (444).
44. For a fuller development of this thesis see Rumsey, "The Development of Character in Kantian Moral Theory," 247–265.
45. For a discussion of Kant's pietistic background and its influence on his work, see Schott, *Cognition and Eros*.
46. Kant, *Observations*, p. 96.
47. Ibid., p. 95.
48. Kant, *Anthropology*, p. 171 (308).
49. Ibid., p. 79 (209).
50. Ibid., p. 167 (303).
51. Ibid.
52. Ibid., p. 172 (309).
53. Ibid., p. 173 (310).
54. Kant, *Metaphysical Elements of Justice*, trans. John Ladd (New York: Bobbs-Merrill, 1965), p. 80 (315). For a full discussion of this issue see Susan Mendus, "Kant: 'An Honest but Narrow-Minded Bourgeois?' " in *Women in Western Political Thought*, eds. Ellen Kennedy and Susan Mendus (New York: St. Martin's, 1987).
55. Kant, *The Metaphysical Elements of Justice*, p. 80 (315).
56. For an interesting discussion of the role of the kindhearted emotions in Kant's moral philosophy see David Cartwright, "Kant's View of the Moral Significance of Kindhearted Emotions and the Moral Insignificance of Kant's View." *The Journal of Value Inquiry* 21 (1987): 291–304.
57. Hume, *Enquiries Concerning Human Understanding and Concerning the Principles of Morals*, ed. L. A. Selby-Bigge (Oxford: Clarendon Press, 1975), p. 172 (137).
58. The gender, race, and class bias of Hume's notion of utility is discussed by Marcia Lind in "Indians, Savages, Peasants, and Women: Hume's Aesthetics," in *Critical Feminist Essays*, ed. Bat Ami Bar-On (State University of New York Press, forthcoming).
59. Hume, *Principles of Morals*, p. 285 (234).
60. Ibid., p. 286 (235).
61. Ibid., p. 181 (144).
62. Ibid., pp. 177, 270 (139, 218).
63. Ibid., p. 271 (220).

64. Hume, *A Treatise of Human Nature*, ed. L. A. Selby-Bigge (Oxford: Oxford University Press, 1978), book III, part III, section I, p. 576.
65. Hume, *Principles of Morals*, p. 178 (141).
66. Ibid., p. 188 (149).
67. This phrase is adapted from Hilary Rose's epistemology, which blends emotion and reason. See her "Hand, Brain, and Heart: A Feminist Epistemology for the Social Sciences," *Signs: Journal of Women in Culture and Society* 9, 1 (1983): 73–90.
68. For an interesting discussion of the response of feminists arguing for equality during the French Revolution to the depiction of woman within the biological sciences, see Joan Wallach Scott, "French Feminists and the Rights of 'Man': Olympe de Gouges's Declarations," *History Workshop* 28 (1989): 1–21.
69. Hume, *Treatise*, book II, part III, section III, p. 415.
70. I am in agreement here with the position of Annette Baier in her essay "Hume, the Women's Moral Theorist?" *Women and Moral Theory*, ed. Eva Feder Kittay and Diana T. Meyers (Savage, MD: Rowman & Littlefield, 1987), that Hume can be characterized as the "woman's moral theorist" in the sense that the type of moral theory described by Hume accords in many ways with the types of conceptions of morality conceived of by women as described by Carol Gilligan in her book *In a Different Voice* (Cambridge: Harvard University Press, 1982). However, I find the question as to Hume's position concerning women and morality far more troubling than does Baier (see below).
71. Hume, *Treatise*, book III, part III, section III, p. 606.
72. Hume, *Principles of Morals*, pp. 269–270 (218). For a detailed discussion of Hume's "hero of feeling" see Donald I. Siebert's excellent book *The Moral Animus of David Hume* (Newark: University of Delaware Press, 1990).
73. Ibid., p. 270 (219).
74. Hume, *Essays: Moral, Political and Literary* (London: Oxford University Press, 1963), p. 132.
75. Ibid., p. 133.
76. Ibid.
77. Ibid., p. 600.
78. Hume, *Principles of Morals*, p. 190 (152).
79. For a discussion of Hume's views on "barbarous" peoples, see Richard H. Popkin, "The Philosophical Bases of Modern Racism," in *Philosophy and the Civilizing Arts*, ed. Craig Walton and John P. Anton (Athens: Ohio University Press, 1974).
80. Hume, *Principles of Morals*, p. 191 (152).
81. Annette Baier, "Good Men's Women: Hume on Chastity and Trust," *Hume Studies* V (1979): 1–19, has employed the following quote to support the position that Hume did not hold sexist views concerning woman's nature: "This sovereignty of the male is a real usurpation, and destroys that nearness of rank, not to say equality, which nature has established between the sexes." *Essays*, p. 188. Christine Battersby, "An Enquiry Concerning the Humean Woman," *Philosophy* 56 (1981): 303–312, notes that the phrase "not to say equality" is grammatically ambiguous, and argues against Baier's use of this passage. My analysis offers support for Battersby's interpretation.
82. Hume, *Principles of Morals*, p. 286 (234).
83. Hume, *Treatise*, book II, part III, section III, p. 417.
84. Ibid., p. 418.
85. Hume, *Essays*, p. 572.

86. Hume, *Treatise*, book II, part II, section XI, p. 394; also see book II, part I, section I, p. 276.
87. Hume, *Essays*, p. 193.
88. Hume, *Treatise*, book II, part II, section X, p. 391.
89. Hume, *History of England*, vols. I–VI (New York: Harper and Brothers, 1850), vol. IV, p. 343.
90. Hume, *History of England*, vol. II, p. 389.
91. Hume, *The Natural History of Religion*, ed. A. W. Clover (Oxford: Clarendon, 1976), p. 37.
92. In this I disagree with Louise Marcil Lacoste's claim in her article "Hume's Position Concerning Women" (*Dialogue* 15 [1976]: 425–440) that Hume viewed the natural virtues as equally distributed between the sexes. In fact I believe that Hume's stance concerning the natural virtues is more revealing of the sexism of his moral theory than his position concerning chastity.
93. Hume, *Treatise*, book III, part II, section XII, p. 573.
94. Ibid., p. 570.
95. Ibid., p. 571, my emphasis.
96. Ibid., p. 572.
97. Hume, *History of England*, vol. II, p. 381.
98. Ibid., vol. IV, p. 343.

Chapter Five

1. For similar analyses of the political theory of Hobbes and Mill see Diana H. Coole, *Women in Political Theory* (Sussex: Wheatsheaf Books, 1988), and Jean Bethke Elshtain, *Public Man, Private Woman* (Princeton: Princeton University Press, 1981).
2. Sir Robert Filmer, *Patriarcha and Other Political Writings of Sir Robert Filmer*, ed. Peter Laslett (Oxford: Basil Blackwell, 1949), p. 241.
3. Although Filmer consistently employed the male pronoun to refer to the king, he did not use patriarchal theory to challenge women's claims to the throne, an omission that was addressed by his critics. See Melissa Butler's "Early Liberal Roots of Feminism: John Locke and the Attack on Patriarchy," *American Political Science Review* 72 (1978): 135–150, especially p. 141.
4. Locke, John, *Two Treastises of Government*, ed. Peter Laslett (New York: Cambridge University Press, 1963), I, 30.
5. Ibid., 29.
6. Ibid., 47.
7. Ibid.
8. Ibid.
9. Ibid.
10. Ibid., II, 4.
11. Ibid., 57.
12. Ibid., 6.
13. Ibid., I, 48.
14. Ibid., II, 78.
15. Ibid., I, 55.
16. Ibid., II, 56.
17. Ibid., 64.
18. Ibid., 82.
19. Ibid., I, 48.

20. Ibid., II, 54.
21. Brennan, Teresa, and Carole Pateman, " 'Mere Auxiliaries to the Common-wealth': Women and the Origins of Liberalism," *Political Studies* XXVII, 2 (1979): 183–200.
22. Locke, *Two Treatises*, II, 74.
23. Ibid., 107.
24. Ibid.
25. Ibid., 72.
26. Ibid., 82.
27. Ibid., 124.
28. See C. B. Macpherson's discussion of this point. *The Political Theory of Possessive Individualism: Hobbes to Locke* (Oxford: Clarendon Press, 1962), pp. 198–199.
29. Locke, *Two Treatises*, II, 85. For further discussion of Locke's views, both written and lived, concerning slavery see James Farr's " 'So Vile and Miserable an Estate': The Problem of Slavery in Locke's Political Thought," *Political Theory* 14, 2 (1986): 263–289.
30. Locke, *Some Considerations of the Consequences of lowering the Interest*, in *The Works of John Locke*, volumes i–x, (London: Thomas Tegg, 1823), vol. v, p. 71.
31. Locke, *The Reasonableness of Christianity*, in *The Works of John Locke*, vol. vii, p. 157.
32. Macpherson, *The Political Theory of Possessive Individualism*, p. 248.
33. Benjamin Rand, ed., Letter to Mrs. Clarke, *The Correspondence of John Locke and Edward Clarke* (Cambridge: Harvard University Press, 1927), pp. 102–103.
34. See Macpherson for a full development of this claim.
35. Locke, *Two Treatises*, II, 7, 4.
36. Ibid., 131.
37. Ibid., I, 47.
38. Ibid.
39. Hegel, *Phenomenology of Spirit*, trans. A. V. Miller (Oxford: Clarendon, 1977), par. 450.
40. Hegel, *Philosophy of Right*, trans. T. M. Knox (London: Oxford University Press, 1967), par. 255.
41. Hegel, *Phenomenology of Spirit*, par., 448.
42. Ibid., par. 457.
43. Ibid., par. 451.
44. Ibid., par. 457.
45. Ibid., par. 450.
46. Ibid., par. 458.
47. Ibid., par. 475.
48. Hegel's *Encyclopedia* is published under the title *Hegel's Philosophy of Nature*, trans. M. J. Petry (London: George Allen and Unwin, 1970).
49. Hegel, *Philosophy of Right*, par. 165.
50. Ibid., par. 166.
51. Hegel, *Hegel's Philosophy of Nature*, section 368.
52. Ibid.
53. Ibid. My discussion of these points has benefited from the excellent analysis offered by Benjamin R. Barber in his "Spirit's Phoenix and History's Owl or The Inco-herence of Dialectics in Hegel's Account of Women," *Political Theory* 16, 1 (1988): 5–28.
54. Hegel, *Philosophy of Right*, par. 166, addition 107.

55. Ibid.
56. Ibid., par. 167–168.
57. Ibid., par. 167.
58. Ibid., par. 169.
59. Ibid., par. 171.
60. For a further discussion of this point see Patricia Jagentowicz Mills, "Hegel and 'The Woman Question': Recognition and Intersubjectivity," in *The Sexism of Social and Political Theory: Women and Reproduction from Plato to Nietzsche*, ed. Lorenne M. G. Clark and Lynda Lange (Toronto: University of Toronto Press, 1979).
61. Hegel, *Philosophy of Right*, par. 33 and 157.
62. Ibid., par. 182, addition 116.
63. Ibid., par. 207.
64. Ibid., par. 260, addition 154.
65. Ibid., par. 147.
66. Ibid., par. 166.
67. Heidi M. Raven, "Has Hegel Anything to Say to Feminists?" *The Owl of Minerva*, 19, 2 (1988): 149–169.
68. Hegel, *Lectures on the Philosophy of Religion*, ed. Peter C. Hodgson, trans. R. F. Brown, P. C. Hodgson, and J. M. Stewart (Berkeley, University of California Press, 1984), vol. 1, p. 205.
69. For a similar argument see Barber's "Spirit's Phoenix and History's Owl."
70. Hegel, *Lectures on the Philosophy of Religion*, vol. 1, p. 46.
71. Hegel, *Hegel's Philosophy of Nature*, section 249.
72. Barber, "Spirit's Phoenix and History's Owl," p. 17. Interestingly, there are different interpretations of the import of this tension within Hegel's philosophy. Barber argues that this tension is inescapable. He explains that once we recognize that for Hegel "the 'Prejudices' of his age are in fact the actuality yielded by history in the epoch of liberation . . . the end not simply of *an* epoch but at the end of the final epoch in which all history had concluded and acquired its definitive meaning," we must conclude that he saw the restriction of women to the family as the rational and necessary consequence of spirit working in history. (20–21.) Contrary to this interpretation, Heidi Ravven argues in "Has Hegel Anything to Say to Feminists?" that the exploitation of women by and for their communities represents a lapse of vision on Hegel's part. She argues that by altering Hegel's assessment of the modern bourgeois state and in particular his acceptance of the family as a subjective harmony and an unexamined, undifferentiated social system, we can find within the Hegelian system "the seeds of a more honest and liberating vision." (164.)

Epilogue

1. *Hypatia: A Journal of Feminist Philosophy* 5, 2 (1990): 11–12.
2. Luce Irigaray, *The Speculum of the Other Woman*, trans. Gillian Gill (Ithaca: Cornell University Press, 1985).
3. Ibid., p. 345.
4. Although some readers of Irigaray have objected to a perceived essentialism within her writings, Diana Fuss persuasively argues that despite the fact that Irigaray "reopens the question of essence and woman's access to it . . . essentialism represents not a trap she falls into but rather a key strategy she puts into play,

not a dangerous oversight but rather a lever of displacement." *Essentially Speaking: Feminism, Nature & Difference* (New York: Routledge, 1989), p. 72.

5. *Feminist Theory and the Philosophies of Man* (London: Croom Helm, 1988), p. 151.

6. See, for example, Susan Bordo, *The Flight to Objectivity* (Albany: State University of New York Press, 1987); Elizabeth Fee, "Is Feminism a Threat to Objectivity?" *International Journal of Women's Studies* 4, 4 (1980); Sandra Harding, *The Science Question in Feminism* (Ithaca: Cornell University Press, 1986); Evelyn Fox Keller, *Reflections on Gender and Science* (New Haven: Yale University Press, 1985); Nancy Tuana, *Feminism & Science* (Bloomington: Indiana University Press, 1988).

7. Nancy Hartsock, *Money, Sex, and Power: Toward a Feminist Historical Materialism* (New York: Longman, 1983); Hilary Rose, "Hand, Brain and Heart: A Feminist Epistemology for the Natural Sciences," *Signs: Journal of Women in Culture and Society* 9, 1 (1983): 73–90, and "Beyond Masculinist Realities: A Feminist Epistemology for the Sciences," in *Feminist Approaches to Science*, ed. Ruth Bleier (New York: Pergamon Press, 1988); Sara Ruddick, *Maternal Thinking: Toward a Politics of Peace* (Boston: Beacon Press, 1989).

8. Sara Ruddick, "Maternal Thinking," in *Mothering: Essays in Feminist Theory*, ed. Joyce Trebilcot (Savage, MD: Rowman and Littlefield, 1983), p. 214.

9. Patricia Hill Collins, "The Social Construction of Black Feminist Thought," in *Black Women in America: Social Science Perspectives*, ed. Micheline R. Malson, Elisabeth Mudimbe-Boyi, Jean F. O'Barr, and Mary Wyer (Chicago: University of Chicago Press, 1990). pp. 299–300.

10. Her analysis is developed in depth in *Black Feminist Thought* (Winchester, MA: Unwin Hyman, 1990).

11. See, for example, debates between "man, the hunter" and "woman, the gatherer" theories of human evolution. For example, see Ruth Hubbard, "Have Only Men Evolved?" in *Biological Woman—the Convenient Myth*, ed. R. Hubbard, M. Henifin, and B. Fried (Cambridge: Schenkman, 1982); and Sarah Blaffer Hrdy, *The Woman That Never Evolved* (Cambridge: Harvard University Press, 1981).

12. Lynn Harkinson Nelson, *Who Knows: From Quine to a Feminist Empiricism* (Philadelphia: Temple University Press, 1990).

13. See, for example, Seyla Benhabib, "The Generalized and the Concrete Other: The Kohlberg-Gilligan Controversy and Feminist Theory," in *Feminism as Critique: On the Politics of Gender*, ed. Seyla Benhabib and Drucilla Cornell (Minneapolis: University of Minnesota Press, 1987), and Virginia Held, "Non-Contractual Society," in *Science, Morality and Feminist Theory*, ed. Marsha Hanen and Kai Nielsen (Calgary: University of Calgary Press, 1987).

14. Carol Gilligan, *In a Different Voice: Psychological Theory and Women's Development* (Cambridge: Harvard University Press, 1982); Nel Noddings, *Caring: A Feminine Approach to Ethics and Moral Education* (Berkeley: University of California Press, 1984); Ruddick, *Maternal Thinking*.

15. For the former point see the writings of Sara Ruddick, for the latter see Virginia Held, "Feminism and Moral Theory," in *Women and Moral Theory*, ed. Eva Feder Kittay and Diana T. Meyers (Savage, MD: Rowman and Littlefield, 1987).

16. Gilligan's study, for example, has been criticized for being based on a study of female students at Harvard and thus arising out of a nonrepresentative sample. Also ethical theories like those of Ruddick which emphasize the mother-child relationship are being criticized for not recognizing the diversity of experiences

of this relationship as well as being criticized by women who are not mothers as not representing their experiences.

17. Wendy Brown, *Manhood and Politics: A Feminist Reading in Political Theory* (Totowa, NJ: Rowman & Littlefield, 1988), p. 12.

18. Ibid., p. 190.

19. Elizabeth Spelman, *Inessential Woman: Problems of Exclusion in Feminist Thought* (Boston: Beacon Press, 1988), p. 14.

BIBLIOGRAPHY

Aiken, Susan Hardy, et al., eds. *Changing Our Minds: Feminist Transformations of Knowledge*. Albany: State University of New York Press, 1988.

Allen, Christine Garside. "Plato on Women." *Feminist Studies II, 2–3 (1975): 131–138*.

Allen, Prudence. *The Concept of Woman: The Aristotelian Revolution 750 BC–AD 1250*. Montreal: Eden Press, 1985.

Andolsen, Barbara Hilkert, Christine E. Gudorf, and Mary D. Pellauer, eds. *Women's Consciousness, Women's Conscience: A Reader in Feminist Ethics*. New York: Winston Press, 1985.

Annas, Julia. "Mill and the Subjection of Women," *Philosophy* 52 (1977): 179–194.

———. "Plato's *Republic* and Feminism." *Philosophy* 51 (1976): 307–321.

The Aprocrypha of the Old Testament. New York: Thomas Nelson and Sons, 1957.

Aquinas, Thomas. *Summa Theologica*. Trans. Fathers of the English Dominican Province. Westminister, MD: Christian Classics, 1981.

Aristotle. *Economics*. Trans. E. S. Forster. In *The Complete Works of Aristotle*. Ed. Jonathan Barnes. Princeton: Princeton University Press, 1984.

———. *Generation of Animals*. Trans. A. Platt. In *The Complete Works of Aristotle*. Ed. Jonathan Barnes. Princeton: Princeton University Press, 1984.

———. *History of Animals*. Trans. d'A. W. Thompson. In *The Complete Works of Aristotle*. Ed. Jonathan Barnes. Princeton: Princeton University Press, 1984.

———. *Metaphysics*. Trans. M. D. Ross. In *The Complete Works of Aristotle*. Ed. Jonathan Barnes. Princeton: Princeton University Press, 1984.

———. *Nicomachean Ethics*. Trans. W. D. Ross. In *The Complete Works of Aristotle*. Ed. Jonathan Barnes. Princeton: Princeton University Press, 1984.

———. *On the Soul*. Trans. J. A. Smith. In *The Complete Works of Aristotle*. Ed. Jonathan Barnes. Princeton: Princeton University Press, 1984.

———. *Parts of Animals*. Trans. W. Ogle. In *The Complete Works of Aristotle*. Ed. Jonathan Barnes. Princeton: Princeton University Press, 1984.

————. *Physiognomonics*. Trans. T. Loveday and E. S. Forster. In *The Complete Works of Aristotle*. Ed. Jonathan Barnes. Princeton: Princeton University Press, 1984.

————. *Politics*. Trans. B. Jowett. In *The Complete Works of Aristotle*. Ed. Jonathan Barnes. Princeton: Princeton University Press, 1984.

————. *Rhetoric*. Trans. W. Rhys Roberts. In *The Complete Works of Aristotle*. Ed. Jonathan Barnes. Princeton: Princeton University Press, 1984.

Arthur, Chris, "Hegel as Lord and Master." *Radical Philosophy 50 (1988): 19–25.*

Baier, Annette C. "Good Men's Women: Hume on Chastity and Trust," *Hume Studies* V (1979): 1–19.

————. "Hume, the Women's Moral Theorist?" *Women and Moral Theory*. Ed. Eva Feder Kittay and Diana T. Meyers. Savage, MD: Rowman & Littlefield, 1987.

Barber, Benjamin R. "Spirit's Phoenix and History's Owl or The Incoherence of Dialectics in Hegel's Account of Women." *Political Theory* 16, 1 (1988): 5–28.

Bar-On, Bat Ami. "Could There Be a Humean Sex-Neutral General Idea of Man?" *Philosophy Research Archives* XIII (1987–88): 367–377.

Battersby, Christine. "An Enquiry Concerning the Humean Woman." *Philosophy* 56 (1981): 303–312.

Bell, Linda A., and Linda Alcoff. "Lordship, Bondage and the Dialectic of Work in Traditional Male/Female Relationships." *Cogito* 2 (1984): 79–93.

Benhabib, Seyla. "The Generalized and the Concrete Other: The Kohlberg-Gilligan Controversy and Feminist Theory." In *Feminism as Critique: On the Politics of Gender*. Ed. Seyla Benhabib and Drucilla Cornell. Minneapolis: University of Minnesota Press, 1987.

————. "On Hegel, Women and Irony." In *Feminist Interpretations and Political Theory*. Ed. Mary Lyndon Shanley and Carole Pateman. University Park, PA: Pennsylvania State University Press , 1991.

Benhabib, Seyla, and Drucilla Cornell, eds. *Feminism as Critique: On the Politics of Gender*. Minneapolis: University of Minnesota Press, 1987.

Bloom, Allan. "Rousseau on the Equality of the Sexes." In *Justice and Equality Here and Now*. Ed. Frank S. Lucash. Ithaca: Cornell University Press, 1986.

Bluestone, Natalie Harris. *Women and the Ideal Society: Plato's Republic and Modern Myths of Gender*. Amherst: The University of Massachusetts Press, 1987.

Blum, Lawrence A. "Kant's and Hegel's Moral Rationalism: A Feminist Perspective." *Canadian Journal of Philosophy* XII, 2 (1982): 287–302.

Bordo, Susan. *The Flight to Objectivity: Essays on Cartesianism and Culture*. Albany: State University of New York Press, 1987.

Boylan, Michael. *Method and Practice in Aristotle's Biology*. Lanham, MD: University Press of America, 1983.

Brabeck, Mary, ed. *Who Cares? Theory, Research, and Educational Implications of the Ethics of Care*. New York: Praeger, 1989.

Brennan, Teresa, and Carole Pateman. " 'Mere Auxiliaries to the Commonwealth': Women and the Origins of Liberalism." *Political Studies* XXVII, 2 (1979): 183–200.

Brown, Wendy. *Manhood and Politics: A Feminist Reading in Political Theory.* Totowa, NJ: Rowman & Littlefield, 1988.

Burns, Steven A. Macleod. "The Humean Female." In *The Sexism of Social and Political Theory: Women and Reproduction from Plato to Nietzsche.* Ed. Lorenne M. G. Clark and Lynda Lange. Toronto: University of Toronto Press, 1979. Pp. 53–59.

Butler, Melissa A. "Early Liberal Roots of Feminism: John Locke and the Attack on Patriarchy." *American Political Science Review* 72 (1978): 135–150.

Canto, Monique. "The Politics of Women's Bodies: Reflections on Plato." In *The Female Body in Western Culture: Contemporary Perspectives.* Ed. Susan Rubin Suleiman. Cambridge: Harvard University Press, 1986. Pp. 339–353.

Cantrell, Carol H. "Analogy as Destiny: Cartesian Man and the Woman Reader." *Hypatia: A Journal of Feminist Philosophy* 5, 2 (1990): 7–19.

Cantrella, Eva. *Pandora's Daughters: The Role and Status of Women in Greek and Roman Antiquity.* Trans. Maureen B. Fant. Baltimore: Johns Hopkins University Press, 1987.

Cartwright, David. "Kant's View of the Moral Significance of Kindhearted Emotions and the Moral Insignificance of Kant's View." *The Journal of Value Inquiry* 21 (1987): 291–304.

Clark, Gillian. *Women in the Ancient World.* London: Oxford University Press, 1989.

Clark, Lorenne M. G. "Women and Locke: Who Owns the Apples in the Garden of Eden?" In *The Sexism of Social and Political Theory: Women and Reproduction from Plato to Nietzsche.* Ed. Lorenne M. G. Clark and Lynda Lange. Toronto: University of Toronto Press, 1979. Pp. 16–40.

Clark, Lorenne M. G., and Lynda Lange, eds. *The Sexism of Social and Political Theory: Women and Reproduction from Plato to Nietzsche.* Toronto: University of Toronto Press, 1979.

Code, Lorraine. *What Can She Know? Feminist Theory and the Construction of Knowledge.* Ithaca: Cornell University Press, 1991.

Code, Lorraine, Sheila Mullett, and Christine Overall, eds. *Feminist Perspectives: Philosophical Essays on Method and Morals.* Toronto: University of Toronto Press, 1988.

Collins, Patricia Hill. *Black Feminist Thought.* Winchester, MA: Unwin Hyman, 1990.

———. "The Social Construction of Black Feminist Thought." In *Black Women in America: Social Science Perspectives.* Ed. Micheline R. Malson, Elisabeth Mudimbe-Boyi, Jean F. O'Barr, and Mary Wyer. Chicago: University of Chicago Press, 1990.

Coole, Diana H. *Women in Political Theory: From Ancient Misogyny to Contemporary Feminism.* Sussex: Wheatsheaf Books, 1988.

Davis, Angela Y. *Women, Race and Class.* New York: Random House, 1981.

Davis, Richard D. "The Conjunction of Property and Freedom in Hegel's Philosophy of Right." *Zeitschrift für philosophische Forschung* 43, 5 (1989): 111–123.

Descartes, René. *Discourse on the Method of Rightly Conducting the Reason.* In *The Philosophical Works of Descartes.* Trans. Elizabeth S. Haldane and G. R. T. Ross. New York: Dover, 1955.

———. *Meditations on First Philosophy.* In *The Philosophical Works of Descartes.* Trans. Elizabeth S. Haldane and G. R. T. Ross. New York: Dover, 1955.

———. *The Passions of the Soul.* In *The Philosophical Works of Descartes.* Trans. Elizabeth S. Haldane and G. R. T. Ross. New York: Dover, 1955.

———. *Rules for the Direction of the Mind.* In *The Philosophical Works of Descartes.* Trans. Elizabeth S. Haldane and G. R. T. Ross. New York: Dover, 1955.

Devereaux, Mary. "Oppressive Texts, Resisting Readers and the Gendered Spectators: The New Aesthetics." *The Journal of Aesthetics and Art Criticism* 48, 3 (1990): 337–348.

Dickason, Anna. "Anatomy and Destiny: The Role of Biology in Plato's View of Women." in *Women and Philosophy.* Ed. C. Gould and M. Wartofsky. New York: Putnam, 1976. Pp. 45–53.

Di Stefano, Christine. *Configurations of Masculinity: A Feminist Perspective on Modern Political Theory.* Ithaca: Cornell University Press, 1991.

Doeuff, Michele le. "Ants and Women, or Philosophy without Borders." *Philosophy* 21, supplement (1987): 41–54.

Donner, Wendy. "Mill on Liberty of Self-Development." *Dialogue* XXVI (1987): 227–237.

duBois, Page. *Centaurs and Amazons: Women and the Pre-history of the Great Chain of Being.* Ann Arbor: University of Michigan Press, 1982.

———. *Sowing the Body: Psychoanalysis and Ancient Representations of Women.* Chicago: The University of Chicago Press, 1988.

Düring, Ingemar. "Aristotle's Method in Biology." *Aristote et les problèmes de methode.* Symposium Aristoteticum, Louvain, Belgium, 1960. Louvain: Centre de Wulf-Mansion, 1980.

Duran, Jane. *Toward a Feminist Epistemology.* Savage, MD: Rowman & Littlefield, 1991.

Easton, Susan M. "Hegel and Feminism." In *Hegel and Modern Philosophy.* Ed. David Lamb. London: Croom Helm, 1987.

Elshtain, Jean Bethke. *Public Man, Private Woman: Women in Social and Political Thought.* Princeton: Princeton University Press, 1981.

Evans, Judith, et al., eds. *Feminism and Political Theory.* London: Sage Publications, 1986.

Ezell, Margaret J. M. *The Patriarch's Wife: Literary Evidence and the History of the Family.* Chapel Hill: University of North Carolina Press, 1987.

Farr, James. " 'So Vile and Miserable an Estate': The Problem of Slavery in Locke's Political Thought." *Political Theory* 14, 2 (1986): 263–289.

Fee, Elizabeth. "Is Feminism a Threat to Objectivity?" *International Journal of Women's Studies* 4, 4 (1980): 378–392.

Filmer, Sir Robert. *Patriarcha and Other Political Writings of Sir Robert Filmer*. Ed. Peter Laslett. Oxford: Basil Blackwell, 1949.

Finlay, M. I. *Ancient Slavery and Modern Ideology*. Hammondsworth: Penguin, 1983.

Flynn, Elizabeth A., and Patrocinio P. Schweickart, eds. *Gender and Reading: Essays on Readers, Texts, and Contexts*. Baltimore: Johns Hopkins University Press, 1986.

Fortenbaugh, W. W. "Aristotle on Slaves and Women." In *Articles on Aristotle*. Vol. 2. Eds. Jonathan Barnes, Malcolm Schofield, and Richard Sorabji. New York: St. Martin's Press, 1977. Pp. 135–139.

Fout, John C. *German Women in the Nineteenth Century: A Social History*. New York: Holmes & Meier, 1984.

Franzwa, Gregg. "The Paradoxes of Equality in the Worlds of Hobbes and Locke." *Southwest Philosophy Review* 5 (1989): 33–37.

Fraser, Antonia. *The Weaker Vessel: Woman's Lot in Seventeenth-Century England*. New York: Knopf, 1984.

Fraser, Nancy. *Unruly Practices: Power, Discourse and Gender in Contemporary Social Theory*. Minneapolis: University of Minnesota Press, 1989.

Fuchs, Jo-Ann Pilardi. "On the War Path and Beyond: Hegel, Freud and Feminist Theory." *Women's Studies International Forum* 6, 6 (1983): 565–572.

Fuss, Diana. *Essentially Speaking: Feminism, Nature & Difference*. New York: Routledge, 1989.

Garry, Ann, and Marilyn Pearsall, eds. *Women, Knowledge and Reality: Explorations in Feminist Philosophy*. Boston: Unwin Hyman, 1989.

Gatens, Moira. "Rousseau and Wollstonecraft: Nature vs. Reason." In *Women and Philosophy*. Ed. Janna L. Thompson. Bundoora, Australia: Australian Association of Philosophy, 1986.

Gates, Henry Louis, Jr. ed. *Black Literature & Literary Theory*. New York: Methuen, 1984.

———. *"Race," Writing, and Difference*. Chicago: University of Chicago Press, 1986.

Gergen, Mary McCanney, ed. *Feminist Thought and the Structure of Knowledge*. New York: New York University Press, 1988.

Gibson, Wendy. *Women in Seventeenth-Century France*. Basingstoke: Macmillan, 1989.

Gilligan, Carol. *In a Different Voice: Psychological Theory and Women's Development*. Cambridge: Harvard University Press, 1982.

Goldstein, Leslie. "Mill, Marx, and Women's Liberation." *Journal of the History of Philosophy* 18, 1 (1980): 319–334.

Gould, Timothy. "Engendering Aesthetics: Sublimity, Sublimation and Misogyny in Burke and Kant." In *Aesthetics, Politics, and Hermeneutics*. Ed. Gerald Bruns and Stephen Watson. Albany: State University of New York Press, 1991.

————. "Intensity and Its Audiences: Notes towards a Feminist Perspective on the Kantian Sublime." *The Journal of Aesthetics and Art Criticism* 48, 4 (1990): 305–315.

Griffiths, Morwenna, and Margaret Whitford, eds. *Feminist Perspectives in Philosophy.* Bloomington: Indiana University Press, 1988.

Grimshaw, Jean. *Philosophy and Feminist Thinking.* Minneapolis: University of Minnesota Press, 1986.

Harding, Sandra. *Whose Science? Whose Knowledge?* Ithaca: Cornell University Press, 1991.

Harding, Sandra, and Merrill B. Hintikka, eds. *Discovering Reality: Feminist Perspectives on Epistemology, Metaphysics, Methodology and Philosophy of Science.* Dordrecht: D. Reidel, 1983.

Harrison, Jonathan. *Hume's Moral Epistemology.* Oxford: Clarendon, 1976.

Hartsock, Nancy C. M. *Money, Sex, and Power: Toward a Feminist Historical Materialism.* New York: Longman, 1983.

Hekman, Susan J. *Gender and Knowledge: Elements of a Postmodern Feminism.* Boston: Northeastern University Press, 1990.

Held, Virginia. "Feminism and Moral Theory." In *Women and Moral Theory.* Ed. Eva Feder Kittay and Diana T. Meyers. Savage, MD: Rowman and Littlefield, 1987.

————. "Non-Contractual Society." In *Science, Morality and Feminist Theory.* Ed. Marsha Hanen and Kai Nielsen. Calgary: University of Calgary Press, 1987.

————. *Rights and Goods: Justifying Social Action.* New York: Free Press, 1984.

Hegel, Georg Wilhelm Friedrich. *Enzyklopädie der philosophischen Wissenschaften im Grundrisse.* Stuttgart: Frommann Verlag, 1956.

————. *Hegel's Philosophy of Nature.* Trans. M. J. Petry. London: George Allen and Unwin, 1970.

————. *Lectures on the Philosophy of Religion.* Ed. Peter C. Hodgson. Trans. R. F. Brown, P. C. Hodgson, J. M. Stewart. Berkeley: University of California Press, 1984.

————. *Phenomenology of Spirit.* Trans. A. V. Miller. Oxford: Clarendon, 1977.

————. *Philosophy of Right.* Trans. T. M. Knox. Oxford: Oxford University Press, 1967.

Henderson, Katherine O. and Barbara F. McManus. *Half Humankind: Contexts and Texts of the Controversy about Women in England, 1540–1640.* Urbana: University of Illinois Press, 1985.

Hesiod. *Theogony, Works and Days, Shield.* Trans. Apostolos Athanassakis. Baltimore: Johns Hopkins University Press, 1983.

Hill, Bridget. *Eighteenth-Century Women: An Anthology.* Boston: Allen and Unwin, 1984.

Hoagland, Sarah Lucia. *Lesbian Ethics: Toward New Value.* Palo Alto, CA: Institute of Lesbian Studies, 1988.

Hodge, Joanna. "Women and the Hegelian State." In *Women in Western Political Philosophy: Kant to Nietzscshe*. Ed. Ellen Kennedy and Susan Mendus. New York: St. Martin's Press, 1987.

Horowitz, Maryanne Clien. "Aristotle and Woman." *Journal of the History of Biology* 9 (1979): 183–213.

Howes, John. "Mill on Women and Human Development." *Australasian Journal of Philosophy* 64, supplement (1989): 66–74.

Hrdy, Sarah Blaffer. *The Woman That Never Evolved*. Cambridge: Harvard University Press, 1981.

Hubbard, Ruth. "Have Only Men Evolved?" In *Biological Woman—the Convenient Myth*. Ed. R. Hubbard, M. Henifin, and B. Fried. Cambridge: Schenkman, 1982.

Hume, David. *Enquiries Concerning Human Understanding and Concerning the Principles of Morals*. Ed. L. A. Selby-Bigge. Oxford: Claredon Press, 1975.

———. *Essays: Moral, Political and Literary*. London: Oxford University Press, 1963.

———. *The History of England, Vols. I–VI*. New York: Harper and Brothers, 1850.

———. *The Natural History of Religion*. Ed. A. W. Clover. Oxford: Clarendon: 1976.

———. *A Treatise of Human Nature*. Ed. L. A. Selby-Bigge. London: Oxford University Press, 1978.

Irigaray, Luce. *The Speculum of the Other Woman*. Trans. Gillian Gill. Ithaca: Cornell University Press, 1985.

Jacobs, Eva, ed. *Women and Society in Eighteenth-Century France*. London: Athlone Press, 1979.

Jaggar, Alison M. *Feminist Politics and Human Nature*. Totowa, NJ: Rowman & Allanheld, 1983.

———. "How Can Philosophy Be Feminist?" *APA Newsletter on Feminism and Philosophy*, April 1988, 4–8.

Jaggar, Alison M., and Susan R. Bordo, eds. *Gender/Body/Knowledge: Feminist Reconstructions of Being and Knowing*, New Brunswick: Rutgers University Press, 1989.

Joeres, Ruth-Ellen B., and Mary Jo Maynes, eds. *German Women in the Eighteenth and Nineteenth Centuries: A Social and Literary History*. Bloomington: Indiana University Press, 1986.

Kant, Immanuel. *Anthropology from a Pragmatic Point of View*. Trans. Mary J. Gregor. The Hague, Netherlands: Martinus Nijhoff, 1974.

———. *Fundamental Principles of the Metaphysic of Morals*. Trans. Thomas K. Abbott. New York: The Liberal Arts Press, 1949.

———. *Grounding for the Metaphysics of Morals*. Trans. James W. Ellington. Indianapolis: Hackett, 1981.

Metaphysic of Morals. In *Kant's Political Writings*. Ed. Hans Reiss, Trans. H. B. Nisbet. London: Cambridge University Press, 1971.

———. *The Metaphysical Elements of Justice*. Trans. John Ladd. New York: Bobbs-Merrill, 1965.

————. *The Metaphysical Principles of Virtue*. Trans. James Ellington. Indianapolis: Bobbs-Merrill, 1964.

————. *Observatons on the Feeling of the Beautiful and Sublime*. Trans. John Goldthwait. Berkeley: University of California Press, 1960.

Keller, Evelyn Fox. *Reflections on Gender and Science*. New Haven: Yale University Press, 1985.

Kennedy, Ellen, and Susan Mendus, eds. *Women in Western Political Philosophy: Kant to Nietzsche*. New York: St. Martin's Press, 1987.

Kittay, Eva Feder, and Diana T. Meyers, eds. *Women and Moral Theory*. Savage, MD: Rowman & Littlefield, 1987.

Kneller, Jane. "Kant's Immature Imagination." In *Critical Feminist Essays in the History of Western Philosophy*. ed. Bat Ami Bar-On. State University of New York Press, forthcoming.

Korsgaard, Christine M. "Kant's Formula of Humanity." *Kantstudien* 77 (1986): 183–202.

Lacoste, Louise Marcil. "Hume's Method in Moral Reasoning." In *The Sexism of Social and Political Theory: Women and Reproduction from Plato to Nietzsche*. Ed. Lorenne M. G. Clark and Lynda Lange. Toronto: University of Toronto Press, 1979. Pp. 60–73.

————. "Hume's Position Concerning Women." *Dialogue* 15 (1976): 425–440.

Landes, Joan B. "Hegel's Conception of the Family." *Polity* 14, 1 (1981): 5–28.

————. *Women and the Public Sphere in the Age of the French Revolution*. Ithaca: Cornell University Press, 1988.

Lange, Lynda. "The Function of Equal Education in Plato's *Republic* and *Laws*." In *The Sexism of Social and Political Theory: Women and Reproduction from Plato to Nietzsche*. Ed. Lorenne M. G. Clark and Lynda Lange. Toronto: University of Toronto Press, 1979. Pp. 3–15.

————. "Rousseau and Modern Feminism." *Social Theory and Practice* 7 (1981): 245–277.

————. "Rousseau: Women and the General Will." In *the Sexism of Social and Political Theory: Women and Reproduction from Plato to Nietzsche*. Ed. Lorenne M. G. Clark and Lynda Lange. Toronto: University of Toronto Press, 1979. Pp. 41–52.

Laqueur, Thomas. "Orgasm, Generation, and the Politics of Reproductive Biology." In *The Making of the Modern Body*. Eds. Catherine Gallagher and Thomas Laqueur. Berkeley: University of California Press, 1987. Pp. 1–41.

Lefkowitz, Mary R., and Maureen B. Fant. *Women's Life in Greece and Rome*. Baltimore: Johns Hopkins University Press, 1982.

Levesque-Lopman, Louise. *Claiming Reality: Phenomenology and Women's Experience*. Totowa: Rowman & Littlefield, 1988.

Lind, Marcia. "Indians, Savages, Peasants, and Women: Hume's Aesthetics." In *Critical Feminist Essays*. Ed. Bat Ami Bar-On. State University of New York Press, forthcoming.

Lloyd, Genevieve. *The Man of Reason: "Male" and "Female" in Western Philosophy*. Minneapolis: University of Minnesota Press, 1984.

———. "Rousseau on Reason, Nature and Women." *Metaphilosophy* 14, 3 and 4 (1983): 308–326.

———. "Selfhood, War and Masculinity." In *Feminist Challenges*. Ed. Carol Pateman and Elizabeth Gross. Boston: Northeastern University Press, 1987.

Locke, John. *Some Considerations of the Consequences of Lowering the Interest*. In *The Works of John Locke*, Volumes I-X. London: Thomas Tegg, 1823.

———. *The Reasonableness of Christianity*. In *The Works of John Locke*, Volumes I-X. London: Thomas Tegg, 1823.

———. *Two Treatises of Government*. Ed. Peter Laslett. New York: Cambridge University Press, 1963.

Lougee, Carolyn C. *Le paradis de femmes: Women, Salons, and Social Stratification in Seventeenth-Century France*. Princeton: Princeton University Press, 1976.

MacCormack, Carol, and Marilyn Strathern, eds. *Nature, Culture and Gender*. London: Cambridge University Press, 1980.

Mackie, J. L. *Hume's Moral Theory*. London: Routledge & Kegan Paul, 1980.

Macpherson, C. B. *The Political Theory of Possessive Individualism: Hobbes to Locke*. Oxford: Clarendon Press, 1962.

Malson, Micheline R., Elisabeth Mudimbe-Boyi, Jean F. O'Barr, and Mary Wyer, eds. *Black Women in America: Social Science Perspectives*. Chicago: University of Chicago Press, 1990.

Martin, Jane Roland. *Reclaiming a Conversation: The Ideal of the Educated Woman*. New Haven: Yale University Press, 1985.

Matthews, Gareth B. "Gender and Essence in Aristotle." In *Women and Philosophy*. Ed. Janna L. Thompson. Bundoora, Australia: Australian Association of Philosophy, 1986.

Mattick, Paul, Jr. "Beautiful and Sublime: Gender Totemism in the Constitution of Art." *The Journal of Aesthetics and Art Criticism* 48, 4 (1990): 293–303.

Meese, Elizabeth. *(Ex)Tensions: Re-Figuring Feminist Criticism*. Urbana: University of Illinois Press, 1990.

Mendus, Susan. "Kant: An Honest but Narrow-Minded Bourgeois?" In *Women in Western Political Philosophy: Kant to Nietzsche*. Ed. Ellen Kennedy and Susan Mendus. New York: St. Martin's Press, 1987. Pp. 21–43.

Meyers, Sylvia Harcstark. *The Bluestocking Circle: Women, Friendship, and the Life of the Mind in Eighteenth-Century England*. Oxford: Clarendon Press, 1990.

Mills, Patricia Jagentowicz. "Hegel and 'The Woman Question': Recognition and Intersubjectivity." In *The Sexism of Social and Political Theory: Women and Re-*

production from Plato to Nietzsche. ed. Lorenne M. G. Clark and Lynda Lange. Toronto: University of Toronto Press, 1979. Pp. 74–98.

———. "Hegel's *Antigone*." *The Owl of Minerva* 17, 2 (1986): 131–152.

———. *Woman, Nature, and Psyche*. New Haven: Yale University Press, 1987.

Mobius, Helga. *Woman of the Baroque Age*. Trans. Barbara Chruscick Beedham. Montclair, NJ: Allanheld & Schram, 1984.

Nelson, Lynn Hankinson. *Who Knows: From Quine to a Feminist Empiricism*. Philadelphia: Temple University Press, 1990.

Newton, Judith, and Deborah Rosenfelt, eds. *Feminist Criticism and Social Change: Sex, Class and Race in Literature and Culture*. New York: Methuen, 1985.

Nicholson, Linda J. *Gender and History: The Limits of Social Theory in the Age of the Family*. New York: Columbia University Press, 1986.

Noddings, Nel. *Caring: A Feminine Approach to Ethics and Moral Education*. Berkeley: University of California Press, 1984.

Nye, Andrea. *Feminist Theory and the Philosophies of Man*. London: Croom Helm, 1988.

Okin, Susan Moller. *Justice, Gender and the Family*. New York: Basic Books, 1989.

———. "Philosopher Queens and Private Wives: Plato on Women and the Family." *Philosophy and Public Affairs* 6, 4 (1977): 345–369.

———. "Women and the Making of the Sentimental Family." *Philosophy and Public Affairs* 11, 1 (1981): 65–88.

———. *Women in Western Political Thought*. Princeton: Princeton University Press, 1979.

Osborne, Martha Lee. "Plato's Unchanging View of Women: A Denial that Anatomy Spells Destiny." *Philosophical Forum* 6, 2–3 (1974): 447–452.

Pateman, Carole. " 'The Disorder of Women': Women, Love, and the Sense of Justice." *Ethics* 91, 1 (1980): 20–34.

———. *The Problem of Political Obligation: A Critical Analysis of Liberal Theory*. New York: John Wiley & Sons, 1979.

———. *The Sexual Contract*. Stanford: Stanford University Press, 1988.

Pateman, Carole and Elizabeth Gross, eds. *Feminist Challenges: Social and Political Theory*. Boston: Northeastern University Press, 1987.

Pearsall, Marilyn, ed. *Women and Values: Readings in Recent Feminist Philosophy*. Belmont, CA: Wadsworth, 1986.

Peradotto, John and J. P. Sullivan, eds. *Women in the Ancient World: The Arethusa Papers*. Albany: State University of New York Press, 1984.

Philo. *Questions and Answers on Exodus*. Trans. Ralph Marcus. Cambridge: Harvard University Press, 1953.

Plato. *Laws*. Trans. A. E. Taylor. In *The Collected Dialogues of Plato*. Ed. Edith Hamilton and Huntington Cairns. Princeton: Princeton University Press, 1961.

———. *Republic*. Trans. Paul Shorey. In *The Collected Dialogues of Plato*. Ed. Edith Hamilton and Huntington Cairns. Princeton: Princeton University Press, 1961.

———. *Symposium*. Trans. Michael Joyce. In *The Collected Dialogues of Plato*. Ed. Edith Hamilton and Huntington Cairns. Princeton: Princeton University Press, 1961.

———. *Timaeus*. Trans. Benjamin Jowett. In *The Collected Dialogues of Plato*. Ed. Edith Hamilton and Huntington Cairns. Princeton: Princeton University Press, 1961.

Popkin, Richard H. "The Philosophical Bases of Modern Racism." In *Philosophy and the Civilizing Arts*. Ed. Craig Walton and John P. Anton. Athens: Ohio University Press, 1974.

Prior, Mary, ed. *Women in English Society, 1500–1800*. New York: Methuen, 1985.

Rand, Benjamin, ed. *The Correspondence of John Locke and Edward Clarke*. Cambridge: Harvard University Press, 1927.

Ravven, Heidi M. "Has Hegel Anything to Say to Feminists?" *The Owl of Minerva* 19, 2 (1988): 149–168.

Rose, Hilary. "Beyond Masculinist Realities: A Feminist Epistemology for the Sciences." In *Feminist Approaches to Science*. Ed. Ruth Bleier. New York: Pergamon Press, 1988.

———. "Hand, Brain, and Heart: A Feminist Epistemology for the Social Sciences." *Signs: Journal of Women in Culture and Society* 9, 1 (1983): 73–90.

Rosen, Stanley. *Plato's Symposium*. New Haven: Yale University Press, 1968.

Rousseau, Jean-Jacques. "A Discourse on the Arts and Sciences." In *The Social Contract and Discourses*. Trans. G. D. H. Cole. New York: E. P. Dutton and Company, 1950.

———. "A Discourse on the Origin of Inequality." In *The Social Contract and Discourses*. Trans. G. D. H. Cole. New York: E. P. Dutton and Company, 1950.

———. *Emile, or On Education*. Trans. Allan Bloom. New York: Basic Books, 1979.

———. *On the Social Contract*. Trans. Judith R. Masters. New York: St. Martin's Press, 1978.

———. *The Social Contract and Discourses*. Trans. G. D. H. Cole. New York: E. P. Dutton and Company, 1950.

Ruddick, Sara. "Maternal Thinking." In *Mothering: Essays in Feminist Theory*. Ed. Joyce Trebilcot. Savage, MD: Rowman and Littlefield, 1983.

———. *Maternal Thinking: Toward a Politics of Peace*. Boston: Beacon Press, 1989.

Rumsey, Jean P. "The Development of Character in Kantian Moral Theory." *Journal of the History of Philosophy* XXVII, 2 (1989): 247–265.

Saxonhouse, Arlene W. "The Philosopher and the Female in the Political Thought of Plato." *Political Theory* 4, 2 (1976): 195–212.

———. *Women in the History of Political Thought: Ancient Greece to Machiavelli*. New York: Praeger, 1985.

Schott, Joan Wallach. "French Feminists and the Rights of 'Man': Olympe de Gouges's Declarations." *History Workshop* 28 (1989): 1–21.

Schott, Robin May. *Cognition and Eros: A Critique of the Kantian Paradigm*. Boston: Beacon Press, 1988.

Schwartz, Joel. *The Sexual Politics of Jean-Jacques Rousseau*. Chicago: University of Chicago Press, 1984.

Shanley, Mary Lyndon. "Marital Slavery and Friendship: John Stuart Mill's *The Subjection of Women*." *Political Theory* 9, 2 (1981): 229–247.

Shanley, Mary Lyndon and Carole Pateman, eds. *Feminist Interpretations and Political Theory*. University Park, PA: Pennsylvania State University Press, 1991.

Shklar, Judith N. *Freedom and Independence: A Study of the Political Ideas of Hegel's Phenomenology of Mind*. London: Cambridge University Press, 1976.

Siebert, Donald T. *The Moral Animus of David Hume*. Newark: University of Delaware Press, 1990.

Siebert, Rudolf J. *Hegel's Concept of Marriage and Family: The Origin of Subjective Freedom*. Washington, D.C.: University Press of America, 1979.

Smith, Janet Farrell. "Plato, Irony, and Equality." *Women's Studies International Forum* 6, 6 (1983): 597–607.

Smith, Nicholas. "Aristotle's Theory of Natural Slavery." *Phoenix* 37 (1983): 109–122.

Sparshott, F. "Aristotle on Women." *Philosophical Inquiry* VII, 3–4 (1985): 177–200.

Spelman, Elizabeth. *Inessential Woman: Problems of Exclusion in Feminist Thought*. Boston: Beacon Press, 1988.

———. Woman as Body: Ancient and Contemporary Views." *Feminist Studies* 1 (1982): 109–131.

Spencer, Samia, ed. *French Women and the Age of Enlightenment*. Bloomington: Indiana University Press, 1984.

Sprenger, Jacob, and Henry Kramer. *Malleus Maleficarium*. Trans. Rev. Montague Summers. London: Pushkin Press, 1948.

Squadrito, Kathy. "Locke on the Equality of the Sexes." *Journal of Social Philosophy* 10 (1979): 6–11.

Suleiman, Susan Rubin, ed. *The Female Body in Western Culture*. Cambridge: Harvard University Press, 1986.

Thompson, Janna. "Women and the High Priests of Reason." *Radical Philosophy* 34 (1983): 10–14.

Tong, Rosemarie. *Feminist Thought: A Comprehensive Introduction*. Boulder: Westview Press, 1989.

Tuana, Nancy, ed. *Feminism & Science*. Bloomington: Indiana University Press, 1989.

———. *The Misbegotten Man: Scientific, Religious, and Philosophical Conceptions of Woman's Nature*, Indiana University Press, forthcoming.

———. "Plato and Feminism" (with William Cowling). *APA Newsletter on Feminism and Philosophy* 90, 1 (1990): 110–115.

———. "Re-Fusing Nature/Nurture." In *Hypatia Reborn*. Ed. Azizah al-Hibri and Margaret Simons. Bloomington: Indiana University Press, 1990.

———. "The Weaker Seed: The Sexist Bias of Reproductive Theory." *Feminism and Science*. Ed. Nancy Tuana. Bloomington: Indiana University Press, 1989.

Vlastos, Gregory. "Was Plato a Feminist?" *Times Literary Supplement* March 17–23, 1989, 725–731.

Wall, Cheryl A., ed. *Changing Our Own Words: Essays on Criticism, Theory and Writing by Black Women.* New Brunswick: Rutgers University Press, 1989.

Weiss, Penny A. "Rousseau, Antifeminism, and Woman's Nature." *Political Theory* 15, 1 (1987): 81–98.

Weiss, Penny, and Anne Harper. "Rousseau's Political Defense of the Sex-Roled Family." *Hypatia: A Journal of Feminist Philosophy* 5, 3 (1990): 90–109.

Winch, Christopher. "Women, Reason, and Education." *Journal of the Philosophy of Education* 19, 1 (1985): 91–98.

Xenophon. *Oeconomicus.* Trans. C. Lord. Ithaca: Cornell University Press, 1970.

INDEX